KANT IN THE LAND OF EXTRATERRESTRIALS

PETER SZENDY

COSMOPOLITICAL PHILOSOFICTIONS
KANT IN THE LAND OF EXTRATERRESTRIALS

Translated by Will Bishop

FORDHAM UNIVERSITY PRESS)) NEW YORK)) 2013

This work was originally published in French as Peter Szendy, *Kant chez les extraterrestres: Philosofictions cosmopolitiques* © 2011 Les Editions de Minuit.

Ouvrage publié avec le concours du Ministère français chargé de la Culture–Centre National du Livre.

This work has been published with the assistance of the French Ministry of Culture–National Center for the Book.

Cet ouvrage a bénéficié du soutien des Programmes d'aide à la publication de l'Institut Français.

This work, published as part of a program of aid for publication, received support from the Institut Français.

Fordham University Press has no responsibility for the persistence or accuracy of URLs for external or third-party Internet websites referred to in this publication and does not guarantee that any content on such websites is, or will remain, accurate or appropriate.

Fordham University Press also publishes its books in a variety of electronic formats. Some content that appears in print may not be available in electronic books.

Library of Congress Cataloging-in-Publication Data

Szendy, Peter.
    [Kant chez les extraterrestres. English]
    Kant in the land of extraterrestrials : cosmopolitical philosofictions / Peter Szendy ; translated by Will Bishop. — First edition.
        pages cm
    Includes bibliographical references.
    ISBN 978-0-8232-5549-8 (cloth : alk. paper) — ISBN 978-0-8232-5550-4 (pbk. : alk. paper)
    1. Kant, Immanuel, 1724–1804.   2. Cosmopolitanism.   3. Science fiction—Philosophy.   I. Title.
    B2799.C82S9413 2013
    193—dc23

                                        2013015250

Printed in the United States of America
15 14 13   5 4 3 2 1
First edition

Áginak
("*il y a dans notre imagination*
un effort pour progresser vers l'infini")
és Karcsinak
("*...és megmutatta mesebeli kincsét/*
az őszi égbolton a tiszta holdat")

CONTENTS

A Little Bit of Tourism . . .

Can you imagine us taking a vacation on the moon?

Can you see us going not to those ever so fond and familiar places, the ones we keep going to every year, or to one of those terrestrial lands we have long since promised ourselves we'd visit, but to an entirely different elsewhere marked by a weightlessness that, for a few memorable days or weeks, would turn us into veritable *cosmopolitans*—citizens of the cosmos?

We can dream about this cosmic exoticism. We can do so all the more inconsequentially given that this vacation would last a limited amount of time and be an utterly provisional abandonment of our terrestrial anchoring with the perfect assurance of our return. A tourist, as is well known, is neither an explorer nor a discoverer. Wherever a tourist goes, the road is already paved; others have gone down it before him; and still others will take it after him.

Today, this *spatial tourism* has become a very serious possibility. A few billionaires have actually already been able to buy themselves a trip into extraterrestrial space. The transporters that propel them beyond our planet are often businesses that were built on the final ruins of the world's bipartition between capitalism and communism: The sorry economic state of the Soviet space station *Mir* led to the foundation of MirCorp, a commercial company that had promised to send the first extra-earthly tourist into space, the American businessman Dennis Tito. (After various difficulties, it was ultimately the company Space Adventures that did so in April 2001, the same company that is currently developing the possibility of going around the moon on the space shuttle *Soyouz* for a hundred million dollars.) For the moment, only several other *happy few* have been able to take this path, but people are already talking of the democratization of these trips beyond our globe.

How many of us will soon be seeking leisure in a hotel sent into orbit? Some, like Robert Bigelow, an American hotel magnate and founder of the Bigelow Aerospace company, have already bought NASA's trademarks for inflatable housing tested in space. Our planet is thus also swelling, expanding beyond its sphere and its atmosphere toward an outside from which it can also look at itself.

What could be more beautiful, what more sublime, it has been said, than the Earth seen from the sky?

)) ((

Even though we recently celebrated the fortieth anniversary of the space mission *Apollo 11,* the famous words of its captain, Neil Armstrong, seem to have become outdated: "That's one small step for a man, one giant leap for mankind," he declared when he placed a foot on lunar ground on July 21, 1969. I was three years old at the time and have no memory whatsoever of having attended the broadcast of this giant little step. A tiny and nonetheless immense if hesitant stride that is now probably destined to be repeated: Following in the footsteps of the first man to walk on the moon is a gesture that will little by little become possible for countless space tourists.

During their visit, they may well pause, with an emotion appropriate to the circumstances, in front of the plaque that the pathbreaking pioneers left on the moon, decorated with the following sentences: "Here Men from the Planet Earth First Set Foot upon the Moon, July 1969 A.D. We Came in Peace for All

Mankind." Perhaps—who knows?—these extra-earthly tourists will also have the opportunity to see enlarged versions of the innumerable "goodwill messages" engraved in miniature on a silicon disc, which—it too left in deposit on the lunar star—still bears the expression of the pacifist intentions of the heads of state from seventy-three earthly countries—among whom figure, haphazardly, the Romanian dictator Nicolae Ceaușescu, the president of Senegal Léopold Sédar Senghor, and Pope Paul VI, prefaced in a way by the declarations of four American presidents. Lyndon B. Johnson's is perhaps the most emblematic: "Space shall be an avenue toward peace."

How will these interplanetary tourists still to come understand words such as "peace" or "mankind"? How will they read these concepts that our predecessors in weightlessness made it a point to engrave into the threshold of the unknown, to leave on what was then the ultimate frontier?

Peace, humankind: These words, or these concepts—as we will see with two major thinkers of the limit, Immanuel Kant and Carl Schmitt—actually border on one another. According to Kant, peace, the true peace that would therefore not be merely a truce between two wars, *perpetual* peace is in effect a regulating ideal that only recedes further out onto the horizon as you think you approach it, as if it could only be thought *at the limit.*[1] And according to Schmitt, humankind as such is that which does not have an enemy, he says, *at least not on this planet,* at least not on Earth: as if the very notion of humankind, in order to be understood or defined, ultimately implied *crossing over the limits* of the Earth.[2]

Humanity, peace: two concepts that refer to each other even as they are constantly sent further away, beyond any existent border. Is their definition or delimitation to be sought beyond their constantly retreating threshold, in the infinite opening of extra-earthliness?

It is this *cosmopolitics just beyond the horizon* that we will be attempting to outline in the following chapters, allowing ourselves to be guided first by Schmitt and then by Kant. Closely reading passages they devoted to the globalization of the earthly globe will allow us to undertake an interplanetary journey to extraterrestrial space that has heretofore gone unexplored. This will also be a way to open our somewhat blasé tourists' eyes[3] by inscribing in the cosmos a radical alterity that we will then have to think anew, as a result, on Earth.

Because this extraterrestrial alterity is not only *out there* and yet to come. It is *already here*: It demands to be read in the philosophical science fictions of Kant and Schmitt. In their *philosofictions* which, like the lunar plaque left by the members of *Apollo 11*, are still awaiting their cosmopolitical readers at the threshold of the unknown.

Readers about whom we know nothing, readers who are other, even *wholly other* [*tout autres*].

)) ((

Kant, to start things off with him, did indeed speak of extraterrestrials. And reading him, we will not be able to avoid wondering: Whom was Kant addressing when he tried to describe those inhabitants of other worlds that allowed him to situate us and *to define us in return*, us humans, us Earthlings, from the point of view of an exteriority to which we do not have access, even if we are already seriously imagining the possibility of colonizing Mars and other planets, perhaps already imagining the *terraformation* that would transform them into inhabitable land?[4]

I remember the faces and the bemused or incredulous smiles in the audience when I happened to pronounce the following sentence in public: Kant did indeed speak of extraterrestrials, I said. One person accused me of wanting to do "sensationalist" philosophy. As if I were secretly dreaming of repeating the panic effect Orson Welles had provoked on October 30, 1938, with his radio adaptation of *The War of the Worlds* as a news bulletin.[5] Others thought that using the great philosophical tradition, I intended to open a front against the "generalized disinformation" or "conspiracy" that they say aims to cover up the innumerable visitations or extraterrestrial abductions that, according to them, are proven. I must admit that I don't really like either of these roles, not any more than I like the role of "the one who doesn't believe." These are worn-out roles, seen time and again in so many films and series, from *The Invaders* to *4400* by way of *Close Encounters of the Third Kind* or *The X-Files*. Can we not imagine another casting and pose the extraterrestrial question differently?

This is what I started to hope when, reading Kant one day, one fine day, I came across passages describing Martians and Venusians with a level of detail that made them almost palpable. To my great surprise, Kant even went so far as to propose a kind of comparative theory or classification of these beings living on other planets, more or less a rational *alienology*. Yet beyond this discovery that I continue to find intriguing, I especially ended up wondering: What in the world drove Kant to speculate like this on forms of life unknown to us, to us Earthlings?

It's true that he is neither the only one nor the first to do so. He is even part of a long-standing philosophical tradition interested in extraterrestrial life that I will sometimes have occasion to mention.[6]

But on the one hand, this particular tradition actually seems to end with him. Hegel, in his *Philosophy of Nature*, affirms that only the planet Earth is "the fatherland [*Heimat*] of spirit" (addition to §280). And beginning with this affirmation, the great line of Western philosophy seems destined to an *anthropogeocentrism* that is hardly disturbed and instead pretty much confirmed by its occasionally being called into question.

On the other hand, and what is most important, when Kant turns to extraterrestrials, he does not do so—or does not only do so—because he is motivated by mere scientific curiosity of an encyclopedic bent. The significance of his speculations, and what makes them more contemporary than ever, is that they are directly and structurally linked to the cosmopolitical stakes of his thinking. In other words, to what we would be tempted today to call *globalization*.[7]

It is as if Kant could sustain a cosmopolitan discourse worthy of its name only by being forced—often in spite of himself, as we will see—to conjure up the extraterrestrial hypothesis. And this is why we will go off on a search for traces of these invaders come from another world even in some of his famous texts where their presence has hardly been noted. (One must admit that they are sometimes very well hidden.)

Yet in order to better measure what awaits us along the way of our Kantian readings, we must consider his writings from a perspective that is resolutely grounded in the contemporary geopolitics of our globalized globe. In other words, if it is true that Kant and his inhabitants of the cosmos speak to us about the limits of our planet Earth and our humanity, if we must still decipher in these philosofictions something of our future hidden in them, we must read them at the risk of being anachronistic. We must come to them from the perspective of the satellites and interplanetary voyages we are familiar with, but also and especially from the perspective of an open question about a new world order that is configured on the basis of the mastery and distribution of the cosmos. From the perspective of what is taking shape under our eyes, then, of a *star wars*.

The major theoretician of this global or globalized order, *the* great thinker of the distribution—earthly and extraterrestrial—of space is certainly Carl Schmitt. This is why, before being able to read what will certainly come off as a strange philosofictive tale called *Kant in the Land of Extraterrestrials,* we will have to take a detour through Schmittian thoughts, especially when they concern *cosmopirates* and conquests of spaces in space.[8]

In short, it is only once we have surveyed the spatial conquests of our time and followed Schmitt in deciphering the international treaties that regulate the exploration of celestial bodies that we will be able to lend an ear to Kant's cosmopolitics and to its indissociable cosmological resonances.

We will then be brought to trace out a final movement. One last gesture that, thanks to a rereading of Kantian thinking about the beautiful and the sublime, will attempt to inscribe into each one of our human, earthly gazes the trembling of a war of the worlds that is already taking place as soon as one opens an eye to see.

Kant's *Critique of the Power of Judgment*, as Hannah Arendt has shown, is in effect immediately political. One could even see in it something like a *hyperpolitics*, in the sense that the political would exceed its traditional limits and its purportedly pure field in order to mark and regulate our very access to the sensible.[9] Yet we might also remember that in Greek, *kosmos* means both the universe and a beautiful decoration, in which case, with Kant and the extraterrestrials that are constantly invading his writing, we are getting ready to take a further step: we need to inscribe a veritable *cosmopolitics* into aesthetics as a *cosmetics*.

CHAPTER 1 *Star Wars*

The Twilight Zone, the television series that started in 1959 and was cut in 1964, was resuscitated in 1985 in color. And it's in one of the episodes from the first new season that you will find the incredible story called "A Small Talent for War." In French, this title was unfaithfully yet interestingly translated as "Risque de paix mondiale," "the danger of world peace."

"A Small Talent for War"

The set for the episode "A Small Talent for War"—a fairly odd set, one must admit—is that of the United Nations in New York. The delegate from the Soviet Union and the delegate from the United States are confronting each other about the intentions of a strange "emissary," an ambassador from elsewhere who brings the threat of the destruction of Earth.

The planet is thus besieged, and this state of exception requires exceptional means or measures. While the Russian is suspicious and demands that preparations for war be undertaken, the American argues for the opposite strategy: "This is the first contact humanity has had with extraterrestrial intelligence," he says. "Do you want them to think we're savages, thinking with our guns instead of . . . ?" He doesn't have time to finish his sentence before the strange emissary from outer space appears in the conference hall of the UN and, before the stunned representatives of

The Twilight Zone: A Small Talent for War (Claudia Weill, 1985)

the human nations, explains that Earthlings have not been up to the task. In the eyes of these aliens that claim to have created life on our planet and overseen the development of our species, we have turned out to be a major disappointment.

How did we disappoint them? Because, as the extraterrestrial says, "You have a small talent for war." This can be understood in two different ways: either as an understatement, in which case we have one heck of a little talent; or else more literally, in which case we are not very good at war or we have only a tiny little gift for armed conflict. Whatever the case may be, according to the ambassador from the other world, we have failed: "And so the experiment is over," he declares. "Within a day, our armada will be in position around your Earth; at that time all life on your planet will be destroyed."

The American delegate objects. He asks for a reprieve of twenty-four hours, which will be granted him. In this tiny lapse

The Twilight Zone: A Small Talent for War (Claudia Weill, 1985)

of time before total destruction, humanity is able to do what it was never able or willing to do up until then: signing what Kant was dreaming about in his 1795 *Perpetual Peace: A Philosophical Sketch*—a treaty for world peace, an agreement for absolute disarmament.

The emissary from the cosmos comes back. "What have you there?" he asks the American delegate. "Peace, Mister Ambassador, peace," the delegate triumphantly answers with hope shining in his eyes. The extraterrestrial starts laughing while everyone echoes his laughter with general or global relief. Yet there was a misunderstanding: What Earthlings had understood as an understatement was actually meant literally by the interplanetary envoi. We humans have never been up to the standards of the wars that were expected of us. "You are woefully backwards in

The Twilight Zone: A Small Talent for War (Claudia Weill, 1985)

the art of war," the representative of the universe declares. "Worst of all, in your hearts you long for peace."

)) ((

This, people will say, is science fiction. It's just entertainment, and we can rest assured that nothing like this will ever happen, at least not while we are alive.

And yet one need only open one's eyes and ears: The form and structure of this fiction is there at work, dictating without a doubt the politics that shape our world.

Ronald Reagan, for example, and in a way that is reminiscent of this *Twilight Zone* episode, addressed the General Assembly of the United Nations in New York on September 21, 1987, in the following way: "Mr. President, Mr. Secretary-General . . . : Let me first welcome the Secretary-General [at the time, Javier Pérez de Cuéllar] back from his pilgrimage for peace in the Middle

East. Hundreds of thousands have already fallen in the bloody conflict between Iran and Iraq."[1] In this context of international conflict—soon to spread once Reagan's successor, George Bush, Senior, launches the Desert Storm operation in January 1991 in the context of the so-called Gulf War and with the approval of the United Nations—Reagan is undertaking a plea for peace, above all else for the free and "democratic" circulation of goods. And he concludes, in the name of the United States: "Can we and all nations not live in peace? In our obsession with antagonisms of the moment, we often forget how much unites all the members of humanity. Perhaps we need some outside, universal threat to make us recognize this common bond. I occasionally think how quickly our differences worldwide would vanish if we were facing an alien threat from outside this world."

It has been said that the program for antimissile defense announced by Reagan in his address to the nation on March 23, 1983—and quickly baptized "Star Wars" by its detractors—was indirectly inspired by science fiction.[2] Yet Reagan's perspective on peace as seen from outer space seems to situate itself beyond political lines since we also find it in his Democratic opponents, as an article by Al Gore called "Moving beyond Kyoto" and published in the July 1, 2007, *New York Times* proves. Gore does not hesitate to cite the conclusion of Reagan's 1987 speech before the General Assembly of the United Nations. He writes:

We—the human species—have arrived at a moment of decision. It is unprecedented and even laughable for us to imagine that we could actually make a conscious choice as a species, but that is nevertheless the challenge that is before us. Our home—Earth—is in danger. What is at risk of being destroyed is not the planet itself, but the conditions that have made it hospitable for human beings. Without realizing the consequences of our actions, we have begun to put so much carbon dioxide into the thin shell of air surrounding our world that we have literally changed the heat balance between Earth and the Sun. This is not a political issue. This is a moral issue, one that affects the survival of human civilization. It is not a question of left versus right; it is a question of right versus wrong. Put simply, it is wrong to destroy the habitability of our planet and ruin the prospects of every generation that follows ours. On Sept. 21, 1987, President Ronald Reagan said, "In our obsession with antagonisms of the moment, we often forget how much unites all the members of humanity. Perhaps we need some outside, universal threat to recognize this common bond. I occasionally think how quickly our differences would vanish if we were facing an alien threat from outside this world." We—all of us—now face a universal threat. Though it is not from outside this world, it is nevertheless cosmic in scale.[3]

Al Gore's plea thus explicitly presents itself as a kind of ecological adaptation of Reagan's Star Wars. In something of the same manner as, in film, the science fiction classic *The Day the Earth Stood Still* (directed by Robert Wise in 1951) was given a 2008 remake (by Scott Derrickson and starring Keanu Reeves): From the first to the second version, the warning extraterrestrials have come to address to us changes, going from the danger of nuclear war to that of the degradation of the environment.

Yet what seems to remain in both cases is the necessity for what is called "the overview effect": a view from "up above," a panoramic view of the Earth as seen from outer space.[4]

)) ((

This plunging view of earthly affairs, this *cosmopolitical* perspective, was of extreme interest to Carl Schmitt. Schmitt was perhaps both its most lucid analyst and critic, in particular when he spoke of a conquest of the cosmos or when he wrote in what was to be his final published text: "Humanity as such and as a whole has no enemies *on this planet*."[5]

But what Schmitt could not or did not want to think about is what ecology intimates when, beyond the earthly discourse of someone like Al Gore, it is already concerned with the refuse of human machines moving through extraterrestrial space.[6] For the cosmos is not and has probably never been merely an *outside*. It is neither an abandoned extraplanetary lot to be used as a junkyard nor a field wide open to conquest as a kind of new New World.[7] Nor is it an eventual refuge, *in fine,* as a long-lasting fantasy would have it, a fantasy that was incarnated in an exemplary way in Rudolph Maté's film *When Worlds Collide* (1951): Faced with the imminent danger of the predicted collision between a giant celestial body and the Earth, a scientist throws himself into a race against the clock to construct a veritable cosmic "Noah's Ark," which, alongside several passengers, will transport samples of objects, animals, and books to their survival elsewhere.[8]

The United Nations Faced with the Cosmos

During the December 13 plenary session in 1958, the first resolution of the United Nations concerning "the peaceful use of outer space"[9] was adopted. Following closely on the launch of the first artificial satellite from Earth (*Sputnik 1* in 1957), the UN aimed to create a special committee charged with the examination in particular of "the nature of legal problems which may arise in the carrying out of programmes to explore outer space."

What was therefore clearly at stake was the constitution of a *law of outer space* whose principles are defined in the resolutions, declarations, and treaties passed over the course of the sixties and seventies. As part of its legal justification, the 1958 resolution already noted the existence of a "common interest of mankind in outer space." The next year, on December 12, 1959, a new resolution that ratified the creation of the "Committee on the Peaceful Uses of Outer Space" notes that "the exploration and use of outer space should be only for the betterment of mankind" while aiming to "avoid the extension of present national rivalries into this new field." But it is only in the December 13, 1963, resolution that one finds the "solemn" proclamation of the following principles:

1. The exploration and use of outer space shall be carried on for the benefit and in the interests of all mankind. 2. Outer space and celestial bodies are free for exploration and use by all States on a basis of equality and in accordance with international law. 3. Outer space and celestial bodies are not subject to national appropriation by claim of sovereignty, by means of use or occupation, or by any other means. . . . 9. States shall regard astronauts as envoys of mankind in outer space, and shall render to them all possible assistance in the event of accident, distress, or emergency landing on the territory of a foreign State or on the high seas.

In 1967, this will also be the basis for the "Treaty on Principles Governing the Activities of States in the Exploration and Use of Outer Space, including the Moon and Other Celestial Bodies."[10] In 1979, these same principles will be affirmed once again with a slight shift of emphasis with only minor differences in the "Agreement Governing the Activities of States on the Moon and Other Celestial Bodies."[11]

Faced with all these resolutions and treaties and the beginnings of *extraterrestrial law*, the Earthling that I am, no specialist in legal questions, cannot help but be surprised. The outer space I thought was virgin and barely explored, the space I thought was free and infinitely open is, legally, already occupied before people have even been able to go into it. In a way, it is *preoccupied* by a legal apparatus that regulates its appropriation in advance: Belonging to humankind as such, there is no way it could become the property of any given state.

Beyond my naïve surprise, there is also, of course, what some analysts of geostrategic issues are already starting to call *Astropolitik*, in other words an astral Realpolitik that has garnered quite a few advocates in the United States. As is attested by the critical studies collected into a remarkable 2009 volume devoted to the question of extraterrestrial security,[12] the geopolitics of the United States since 1990 has been marked by the unilateral quest for exclusive control over the cosmos. Ever more conscious of the importance of controlling the Earth's satellites, military strategists and advisers under the presidencies of both Bill Clinton and George W. Bush repeatedly affirmed the necessity of the "full spectrum dominance" of space on behalf of the United States.[13]

Whatever the outcome is for the star wars currently under preparation, whether humankind will be a mere figurehead for an empire capable of occupying extraterrestrial space or will share in the enjoyment of its benefits, one question remains unanswered.

This question comes to us from Carl Schmitt, and it is a question he confided in its simplest and perhaps freest form to the journal he kept after the Second World War over the course of the years when he was interrogated and judged at Nuremberg for complicity with the Nazi regime. In his *Glossarium* on November 5, 1947, one can read (if one indeed chooses to read):[14]

There can be no movement without empty space. There is also no law without free space [*kein Recht ohne freien Raum*]. Any seizing or regular delimitation of space necessitates a free space that remains outside, beyond the law [*erfordert einen draussen, ausserhalb des Rechts verbleibenden freien Raum*]. Freedom is the freedom to move, and there is no other. How terrifying is a world where there is no foreign land [*Ausland*] but only inner territory [*Inland*]; no path toward the open [*kein Weg ins Freie*]; no leeway [*Spielraum*] where forces are freely measured and experienced.

Is this the world we live in? Is globalization, a becoming-world of the world, our unprecedented experience of this? Is the historical moment that brings us to touch on the limits of the globe inextricably the moment that will have already closed off and foreclosed exteriority or the extra-earthly by making it already now and forever more the domain of humanity?

In 1950, in the preface to his *Nomos of the Earth*, Schmitt
wrote:

The traditional Eurocentric order of peoples' law [*Völkerrecht*]
is foundering today. . . . This order arose from a legendary and
unforeseen discovery of a new world [in other words, Amer-
ica], from an unrepeatable historical event. Only in fantastic
parallels [*in phantastischen Parallelen*] can one imagine a
modern recurrence, such as men on their way to the moon dis-
covering a new and hitherto unknown planet [*einen neuen,
bisher völlig unbekannten Weltkörper*] that could be exploited
freely and utilized effectively to relieve their struggles on earth
[*zur Entlastung ihres Erdenstreites*].[15]

These were the terms Schmitt used to note the disappearance
of the essentially European order that, after the discovery of the
American continent, had regulated earthly geopolitics for four
centuries. But by diagnosing the end of a certain division (*nomos*)
of the planet Earth, Schmitt, in 1950, did not yet seriously imagine
that the beginnings of a new world order could rely on real extraterrestrial conquests: The issues of the coming world, he thought,
will be resolutely earthly. They will be negotiated not by having
one's head in the stars but with one's feet on Earth.

The question of a new *nomos* of the Earth will not be answered
with such fantasies [*Phantasien*], any more than it will be with
further scientific discoveries. Human thinking again must be
directed to the elemental orders of its terrestrial being here
and now [*auf die elementaren Ordnungen ihres terrestrisches
Daseins*]. (*Nomos*, 39)

It is, however, in all seriousness, and no longer "in fantastic
parallels," that Schmitt, in 1962, considered the question of a division [*nomos*] of the cosmos that makes earthly affairs suddenly
seem secondary.

New incommensurable spaces [*neue unermessliche Raüme*] are opening to us and, as it always happens whenever human activity is concerned, these spaces will be appropriated and distributed [*genommen und geteilt*] in one way or another. For a while now, we have been speaking of a nomos of the Earth. Today, the problem extends to infinity, leading us to the need to think of a nomos of the cosmos. Compared to the enormous proportions of the appropriation and division of cosmic space, the historical events of the past—appropriations of earth, sea, and even the conquest of aerial space—seem small and insignificant.[16]

Yet if it is true, as Schmitt noted in his *Glossarium*, that any legal order presupposes some kind of remains—a space of freedom that escapes it—how might the cosmos play this role and thus allow for the eventual instauration of a new *nomos* if it is already entirely occupied by humanity as such?

We need to treat this question to its fullest extent, first by following Schmitt when he traces out the history of the appropriations that have punctuated the globalization of the globe, then when he analyzes the emergence of humanity as a subject of a new state of law.

Appropriation and Distribution of Space

If there is a truly central concept to Schmitt's approach to issues in geopolitics and international law, it's *nomos*. As he writes in the introductory considerations that open his great 1950 book, *The Nomos of the Earth*: "The Greek word . . . for the first land appropriation understood as the first partition and classification of space, for the original division and distribution, is *nomos*."[17] Since Plato, the word *nomos* has been most often understood as signifying law, norm, or rule. Yet Schmitt would like to return to it a sense he would like to be able to call original, tied to "land appropriation" (69). As he further explains in a 1953 article that forms a kind of later "corollary" to *Nomos of the Earth*,[18] it is from this *concretely earthly* anchoring that stem two other meanings of the same term: After the initial and foundational appropriation comes "original distribution" (*Ur-Teil*) and then the use or management of the land for "production." In short, Schmitt concludes:

> In every stage of life, in every economic order, in every period of legal history until now, things have been appropriated, distributed, and produced. Prior to every legal, economic, and social order are these elementary questions: *Where and how was it appropriated? Where and how was it divided? Where and how was it produced?* (*Nomos*, 327–28)

This triple question seems to furnish a kind of algebra that allows for a simple characterization of different geopolitical movements in history: Imperialism, for example, is redefined as "the precedence of appropriation before distribution" (330). Yet at the very moment he concludes his brief meditation on the three meanings of *nomos*, Schmitt is most concerned with "the current state of world unity" (335, translation modified)—in other words, with globalization once it reaches its limit and its end: "Has humanity today actually 'appropriated' the earth as a unity, so that there is nothing more to be appropriated? Has appropriation really ceased? Is there now only division and distribution? Or does only production remain?" (335). The answer to these questions is perhaps to be found, as we shall see, outside terrestrial space, outside the earthly atmosphere.

But let's not proceed too quickly; let's not get in a rush and act as if it were but one small step to go from the *nomos* of the Earth to the *nomos* of the cosmos. For the catch, capture, or appropriation [*la prise, la saisie ou l'appropriation*] in Schmitt's thinking is subject to many other modalities and developments that we need to take into consideration.

Let's start again.

)) ((

Alongside land appropriations, only some of which found a new geopolitical order,[19] there are other spaces that can be appropriated.

First the land, then the sea, and then the air. And so on and so forth, etc., one would like to be able to say. Yet, on the one hand, it is quite precisely the limit or end of this series that is our question. And on the other hand, the *telluric* at the origin of the series will always be privileged in Schmitt's work.

This can be heard in an almost naïve tonality in a kind of geopolitical tale that Schmitt, as the dedication puts it, "told to [his] daughter Anima."

> Man is an earthly being [*Landwesen*]; he walks on land [*Landtreter*]. He stands, walks, and moves on the firm earth. This is his standpoint and his ground [*sein Standpunkt und sein Boden*] and this is what gives him his point of view [*Blickpunkt*]; it is what determines his impressions and his way of seeing the world. . . . The star on which he lives he thus names the "Earth," even if we know very well that its surface is made of almost three-fourths water and only one-fourth earth, the vastest of its continents being no more than floating islands. Since the moment we learned that this Earth of ours is shaped like a sphere, we have spoken, as if it were clearly obvious, of the "terrestrial globe" [*Erdball*], of the "earthly sphere" [*Erdkugel*]. You would have trouble imagining a "marine globe" [*Seeball*], a "maritime sphere" [*Seekugel*].[20]

The sea, unlike the earth, as Schmitt will write several years later in *Nomos of the Earth,* "knows no such apparent unity of space and law, of order and orientation."[21] The sea is thus essentially "free" (*frei*) because it harbors no "trace" (*Spur*) of the ships that cross it, since nothing can be engraved or inscribed in it. Inappropriable in and of itself, the sea is first of all "a free zone of free booty" (*ein freies Feld freier Beute*, 43, translation modified), the realm of piracy and all kinds of banditry.

And yet, with the birth of the great sea empires that Schmitt calls "thalassocracies," the sea itself is submitted to an order. It becomes the theater of "sea appropriations" (*Seenahmen*), that is to say that it is subjected to the domination of the geopolitical entity that has the strongest technical mastery of it, which was, as is well known, long the case of England. These appropriations of the marine element are nonetheless entirely different from those of the earth; and this is in fact why debates on marine legislation have provided inspiration for laws on extraterrestrial space, just as the vocabulary of maritime navigation still furnishes ordinary language with the obligatory metaphors and catachreses that allow us to speak of moving through the cosmos.[22]

Schmitt thus considers the sea and the earth as two "separate and distinct worlds."[23] Two worlds that are opposed to each other on the surface of our globe (that *globus terraqueus*, as Kant wrote in §62 of his *Doctrine of Law*), two elements whose opposition has structured the Europocentric *nomos* of our planet up until its destruction shortly before the era when Schmitt, not without a certain nostalgia, wrote *The Nomos of the Earth*.

Yet this *nomos*—whose foundation, we must not forget, was the existence of a reserve of free space available for conquest—this stable geopolitical order was also, for Schmitt, an apparatus [*dispositif*] for limiting war, a way of circumscribing it or giving it a context through the mutual recognition of belligerent states. I'll be returning to this question in the next chapter when we'll read the way Schmitt analyzes humanitarian pacifism. The fact remains that, as is often the case in Schmitt's work, it is situations of war that allow us to grasp the earth's articulation with the sea, that is to say their equilibrium as border zones, up until the invention of aerial warfare.

Thus when a harbor is blocked or a coastal city is bombarded, war can "act directly on the land from the sea, but effectively applying the specific means of sea war to land" (*Nomos*, 312, translation modified). Yet this "collision of land war and sea war" was limited to "the fringes" (*am Rande*) of the two spheres. It does not call into question what makes them fundamentally distinct from one another; it does not undermine their *purity*.[24] Within the *nomos* structured this way, armed confrontations and conflicts occur according to what Schmitt describes as "warring parties fac[ing] each other *on the same plane*" (319): Adversaries are *co-present* in a homogeneous theater of operations, in the same territory that carries them and places them with the *one facing the other.*

For Schmitt, it is aviation's conquest of airspace and air warfare that radically overthrows this "horizontal confrontation" (*Nomos*, 319). It overthrows it entirely because air war has "no theater [*Schauplatz*] and no spectators." Now that it no longer happens in a theater where adversaries can appear and be present together, confrontation has lost its *front*, just as it does not have a *horizon*.[25]

In 1950, *Nomos of the Earth* concludes with this abolition of the flatness of war and its anchoring in the ground. And we may wonder what in the world remains of the very idea of *nomos* when what Schmitt called the "terrestrial fundament, in which all law is rooted" (47) is lost.

)) ((

In fact, in his later texts, we witness a double gesture: On the one hand, Schmitt reaffirms the founding telluric link, as if its imminent rupture nourished the desire to cling to it; and, on the other hand, he extends the triple meaning of *nomos* (appropriation, distribution, and productive exploitation) to increasingly abstract or unearthly elements and matters.

Published in 1962, *The Theory of the Partisan* oscillates in a striking way between these two poles: the affirmation of a "specifically terrestrial type of active fighter" and considerations of how he has been "disoriented" by "motorization." "A motorized partisan loses his telluric character," writes Schmitt; "he leaves his own turf" even though he is one of "the last sentinels of the earth [*einer der letzten Posten der Erde*] as a not yet completely destroyed element of world history."[26] This hesitation about the Earth—one clings to it and then leaves it; one distances oneself from it and returns to it—this pendulum movement between earthing and de-earthing culminates and finds its greatest expanse in Schmitt's consideration of extending the figure of the partisan to a cosmic scale. This *cosmopartisan*, having traveled so far away from his mother planet, is nonetheless struggling *for the earth*.

> Our problem is widened to . . . planetary dimensions. It even reaches still further to supraplanetary regions [*ins Über-Plane-tarische*]. Technological progress makes possible the journey into cosmic spaces, and thereby opens up equally immeasurable new possibilities for political conquests. In fact, the new spaces can and must be conquered [*genommen*] by men. Old-style land- and sea-appropriations [*Land- und Seenahmen*], as known in the previous history of mankind, will be followed by new-style space-appropriations [*Raumnahmen*]. . . . Only he who dominates an earth that has become so tiny will be able to appropriate and to utilize [*nehmen und nutzen*] new spaces. Consequently, these immeasurable spaces also become potential battlefields [*potentielle Kampfräume*], and the domination of this earth hangs in the balance. The famous astronauts and cosmonauts, who formerly were only propaganda stars of the mass media (press, radio, and television), will have the opportunity to become cosmopirates [*Kosmopiraten*], even perhaps to morph into cosmopartisans [*Kosmopartisanen*]. (Schmitt, *Partisan*, 80)

In a gesture analogous to one we'll see Kant make, the greatest distance from the planet Earth is immediately followed by repatriation and re-earthing: Whatever sidereal distance may separate them from our globe, Schmitt seems to be saying, cosmocombatants of all kinds will always be battling in relation to terrestrial power struggles.

It really does seem that we have trouble letting go and entering into weightlessness without ensuring ourselves of at least a symbolic earthbound gravitation. What is Schmitt afraid of here—and, in all likelihood, what is our fear, we Earthlings, as we read him? It may be that we tremble at the idea that in leaving our planet, we may also be breaking all our ties to the high value of presence: How many science fiction movies, from Kubrick's famous *Space Odyssey* to Andrei Tarkovsky's or Steven Soderbergh's *Solaris*, stage the confines of the cosmos as the place where we can no longer tell the difference between yesterday, today, and tomorrow?[27]

Yet the case remains that for Schmitt "the conquest of the cosmos is purely future" (*pure Zukunft*), as he put it in 1962.[28] In other words, it remains *purely* to come, it is *purely* opposed to the present—which it thus installs in its stable presence—in the same way that *purely terrestrial* war and *purely maritime* war were opposed in *Nomos of the Earth*. The purity of these oppositions is no doubt quite precisely what keeps us from thinking that the *nomos* of the cosmos is not merely waiting in the future, but that it is already there, that it emerges and retreats from the past and allows us to grasp *ourselves* as humankind.

Yet as we read Schmitt, let us at least provisionally accept being led back to earth, to presence or co-presence on our planet Earth, to the terrestrial and the earthly as the foundation for and anchoring of law—in other words, of any lasting possibility of appropriation and distribution. Let us accept this, for it is precisely by following this movement of Earthling repatriation that we will be able to see planet Earth exhaust itself and the *globus terraqueus* globalize itself to the point where there is "nothing more to be appropriated."[29]

As it happens, in his very last text from 1978, Schmitt performs a gripping historical shortcut, delivering a vertiginously deep perspective on the shift from sea appropriation (*Seenahme*) to what he calls "industry appropriations" (*Industrienahmen*). Once these appropriations become "planetary," they allow for the "appropriation of world space" (*Weltraumnahme*).[30] One last appropriation, then, an ultimate capture—that of globalization itself—which, according to Schmitt, signifies the end of politics, that is to say its dissolution into a worldwide police force in the service of the economy.[31]

)) ((

The question that stays with us, with us Earthlings who still inhabit this *globus terraqueus,* the question that haunts us *after* globalization (an after that is precisely not a pure future, but that also comes to us from *before*) is thus that of a *new* spatial order. This order, if one accepts the fact that it is coming, is probably announced somehow in the way the past returns. In other words, in the constitution of what was, according to Schmitt's reading of world history, the *nomos* of the Earth for four hundred years: a global geopolitical order that resulted from the "circumnavigation of the earth and the great discoveries of the 15th and 16th centuries."[32] If we want to potentially understand something about what awaits us *after* its dissolution—whether this after has or does not have the form of another *nomos*—we need to study the conditions of its formation—in other words, what, in Schmitt's logic, allows in general for a *nomos* to be constituted.

As we read in Schmitt's *Glossarium,* there is not, for him, any possibility of law "without free space"; there is no "seizing or regular delimitation" without "a free space that remains outside, beyond the law." This may well be the primary foundation for what Schmitt calls a *nomos:* the distribution between a zone of law and a no-law zone, between its inside and its outside. In effect, as he writes in *Nomos of the Earth*:

> There are two different types of land-appropriations [*Landnahmen*]: those that proceed *within* a given order of international law, which readily receive the recognition of other peoples, and *others*, which uproot an existing spatial order and establish a new *nomos* of the whole spatial sphere of neighboring peoples.

A land-appropriation occurs with every territorial change. But not every land-appropriation, not every alteration of borders, nor even every founding of a new colony . . . is a process that constitutes a new *nomos*. In particular, it depends upon whether there is free land to be had [*ob ein Spielraum freien Bodens vorhanden ist*]. (82)

If every *nomos*, defined as the appropriation, distribution, and exploitation of a given space, is essentially the equilibrium of a global spatial arrangement (in other words, a stable geopolitical structure), we can understand that its foundation demands a possibility for movement that is not already included in the preexisting order. The institution of a new *nomos* implies, as the German term *Spielraum* indicates, a space where there is room to maneuver, where there is some *play*. Where things can move, tremble, and come apart.

This is why, when he attempts to analyze the birth of the geopolitical order that was set up little by little starting with the discovery of America in 1492, Schmitt insists on what he calls an "essential and decisive factor for the following centuries": "The emerging new world did not appear as a new enemy, but as *free space,* an area open to European occupation and expansion" (87, translation modified). We could find countless other formulations of this same logic in *The Nomos of the Earth*: It is the existence of a space freely open to appropriation that allows for an order to be initiated and made stable, an order to which that space remains exterior.[33] In short, for there to be a *nomos*, an *anomal* outside must subsist that is nonetheless a part of this very *nomos* since it is its condition of possibility.

Yet what is such a space *free of law* whose existence opens the possibility for the emergence of a new world order? It is fundamentally an *empty* space. And, as Schmitt forcefully affirms in the geopolitical fable he told to his daughter, *there has not always been* empty space (in the same way that, as we shall see, it is not certain that such space still exists):

Copernicus was the first to prove scientifically that the Earth rotates around the Sun. . . . His *De revolutionibus orbum coelestium* dates from 1543. He certainly did thus transform our solar system, but he was still attached to the idea that the universe in its entirety [*Weltall*], the cosmos, is a limited [*begrenzt*] space. The world, in the sense of the great cosmos, and thus the very notion of space were not yet transformed. Barely a few decades later, the borders fell. In the philosophical system of Giordano Bruno, the solar system, at the heart of which the Earth moves as a planet around the Sun, is but one of the numerous solar systems of the infinite firmament. Following on the scientific experiments of Galileo, these philosophical speculations became a mathematically demonstrable truth. Kepler calculated the planets' trajectories, even if he, too, trembled when he thought about the infinity of these spaces where planetary systems move without imaginable borders or center. With Newton's theory, the new concept of space was established for all of Enlightenment Europe to see. Stars, masses of matter, move to the extent that forces of attraction and repulsion are balanced and according to laws of gravity in infinite and empty space. Men could thus henceforth imagine empty space, something that wasn't the case before.[34]

There are certainly many shortcuts in this tale that sounds like a fable. But what is important for us is the logic of the whole: the birth, in the West, of the idea of an empty cosmic space. For this is the event that, for Schmitt, makes possible what he calls "the first authentic revolution of space," the one that, for the first time, placed "the veritable earthly globe in its entirety as a sphere" (*Nomos,* 64–65) into human hands:

> The change [*Veränderung*] contained in the idea of empty and infinite space cannot be explained as the simple consequence of a purely geographical extension of the Earth known up until

that point. It is so fundamental and revolutionary that one could just as well claim the opposite, that the discovery of new continents and the circumnavigation of the Earth were but the manifestations and consequences of more profound mutations. This is the only reason why landing [*Landung*] on an unknown island was capable of inaugurating the whole era of discovery. Often, men from the West or the East landed in America. The Vikings, as we know, had already found [*gefunden*] North America when they came from Greenland around the year 1000. . . . A spatial revolution presupposes more than a landing in a country theretofore unknown. It presupposes a transformation of the notion of space encompassing all levels and domains of human existence. (*Nomos*, 67–68)

Schmitt performs a kind of revolution within revolution here: The spatial revolution that stems from the discovery of a new continent is only a revolution if placed against the backdrop of the cosmological revolution (the one in Copernicus's *De revolutionibus* and of his successors) that preceded it and made it possible. The cosmos, as a paradigm of empty space, was thus already there; its discovery preceded and conditioned the revolution of earthly space, in other words, the institution of the first truly global or globalized order on Earth. The invention of the void in the cosmos will thus, according to Schmitt, have allowed for the discovery of the free space that, on planet Earth, will have in turn made the institution of a *nomos* possible.

)) ((

And what is our situation today? How might spatial conquest and star wars provide the background and backdrop for the invention of a new world order, perhaps a new *nomos*, one whose coming was so intensely sought out by Schmitt?

If we have no simple answers to these questions, it's because, as Schmitt wrote in a passage from his preface to *Nomos of the Earth* that we have already cited, the "unforeseen discovery of a new world" is "an unrepeatable historical event" (39). Since then, in effect, many other radical changes have taken place. The flatness of the face-to-face confrontation that could exist on earth or on the sea was irremediably complicated by submarine and aerial war. And the disappearance of the level space of co-presence was accompanied by an exhaustion of the globe, subjected to planetary appropriations of industry that are veritable worldwide appropriations of space.

We can thus now wonder if a free space is still possible as the very condition of *nomic* appropriation and distribution and as a prelude to the institution of a new geopolitical structure. Empty space, that negative side, or verso of a recto that might be named *presence*, is perhaps in crisis; it is perhaps moribund, as would also be, as a consequence, the very notion of *nomos*. Not only because we may suspect, as Schmitt does, that everything has already been appropriated on Earth, so much so that there would no longer be any *res nullius* on our planet, no longer any domain available for a future capture, but also because that space that is par excellence free—the cosmos, that paradigm for all other spaces open to appropriation—has already been occupied, is *preoccupied* by humanity as such.

It is, say the jurists, *res communis humanitatis*.

Humanity Raises the Anchor

"To make of the planet we inhabit, to make of the Earth itself, a spaceship," wrote Schmitt in 1955 when speaking of the technical expansion of the cosmos.[35]

Taken out of its immediate context (a debate over Ernst Jünger's then recent book *The Gordian Knot*), this phrase certainly makes for a gripping image and powerful figuration of the technical power Schmitt describes as "raging," and that might well allow humans to leave their earthly anchor, taking their planet, their conditions of living, and their atmosphere away to an elsewhere.[36] Yet by saying "we," this sentence also poses a question better than many other discourses are able to: *What is humanity?*

This is a question that, as we will soon see with Kant, cannot be posed in all rigorousness unless we detach ourselves from the Earth. It is not here or there but *out there* that we can ask *ourselves*: Who are we?

Yet before we undertake with Kant an interstellar journey that, in a way, has *already taken place*, before we transport ourselves toward that extraterrestrial limit where humanity *will have been a question,* we need to prolong our stay on Earth. To watch the progressive destitution of a *nomos* that, as it loses its foundational telluric tie, seems precisely to allow humanity to emerge as a new geopolitical subject.

In *Nomos of the Earth*, Schmitt devotes several important pages to the dissolution between 1890 and 1918 of the Eurocentric order that had regulated our planet. And it's a dissolution that leads, he says, to a loss of the substance of world space, or rather, and more precisely, to what he calls "the spacelessness of a general universalism [die Raumlosigkeit eines allgemein Universalen]" (230). Strangely, if this is a nonspace, it is both because it has been deprived of its content and because it is too full: It is in effect emptied of its previous content, since its emergence coincided with the affirmation of an "international community" that, in principle or in law, tolerates borders less and less; but it is also saturated in advance since "still not effectively occupied state areas" (235) no longer exist.

The abstraction of this universal space, which signifies the disappearance of the former *nomos* born from the discovery of America while it prepares the grounds for humanity's entrance as a geopolitical subject, is thus also the moment when there is no longer any free space available for land appropriation. As Schmitt writes with great lucidity in a passage that has lost none of its incisiveness today, this means quite simply that the regime of appropriation is no longer telluric, tied to the ground, but is linked to industry appropriations (*Industrienahmen*) that, as you'll remember, prepare for the appropriation of world space (*Weltraumnahmne*) on a planetary scale:

> The prevailing concept of a global universalism lacking any spatial sense [*eines raumlos globalen Universalismus*] certainly expressed a reality in the economy distinct from the state—an economy of free world trade and a free world market [*ein freier Welthandel und Weltmarkt*], with the free movement of . . . capital and labor. (*Nomos*, 235)

One of the important historical phases in the evolution toward this "empty space open to socio-economic processes" (252, translation modified) is, for Schmitt, the birth of "intervention treaties in international law," like those the United States signed in 1903 with Cuba and Panama. For with these treaties, it is no longer a question of colonization or territorial annexation:

> The external, emptied space of the controlled state's territorial sovereignty [*der äussere, entleerte Raum der territorialen Souveränität*] remains inviolate, but the material content of this sovereignty is changed. . . . Political control and domination were based on intervention, while the territorial *status quo* remained guaranteed. The controlling state had the right to interfere in the affairs of the controlled state in order to protect independence or private property, maintain order and security, preserve the legitimacy or legality of a government or for any other reason, at its own discretion. (*Nomos*, 252, translation modified)

Today, how many states are "controlled" in this way even as they maintain a semblance of sovereignty that precisely *seems* intact? From Iraq to Afghanistan, there is certainly no lack of examples. Whatever the case may be, the emptiness of such a space is, for Schmitt, entirely different from the emptiness of the cosmos or from that of the new world discovered in 1492. Schmitt seems to conceive of these spaces as *authentically or naturally free*, whereas Cuba and Panama are, in 1903, *artificially emptied* of their content, their territory remaining theirs only in a purely formal or formalist sense of property.

However much credit one chooses to lend to this opposition, what Schmitt is thus describing are the premises of what we confusedly call globalization, which cannot be defined as a mere extension of known earthly space, as was the case just after the great circumnavigations that gave birth to a planetary geopolitical representation that Schmitt qualifies as the "concept of global lines [*Globales Liniendenken*]" (*Nomos*, 90).[37] In this sense, nothing becomes global in globalization, which is instead the indifferentiation or the emptying out of an already appropriated and distributed global space.

)) ((

This *hollow* spatiality, as we might call it, *is further dug out* in Schmitt's narrative by what he calls "the failure of the Geneva Protocol." This is the appellation he uses to name the League of Nations in which Kant foresaw an institution capable of incarnating the "perfect political unification" of humanity. We will come to this, and we will have to read and reread the texts Kant devoted to cosmopolitanism and to the project for perpetual peace. The fact remains that for Schmitt, humanity, once it emerges as a category in international law, contributes to emptying "concrete space" of any substance: As the "universalist principle" extends "to all of Earth and humanity," it leads "to the intervention of everyone in everything."[38]

Of course, recourse to the notion of humanity does not date from the creation of the League of Nations, as Schmitt himself admits, particularly in the pages of *Nomos of the Earth* where he retraces the different forms of justification for the *conquista* of the new world (starting on 101). But the modern humanitarianism of the League of Nations is particular in Schmitt's eyes insofar as it leads to a transformation of "war itself" by turning it into "an 'offense' in the criminal sense."[39] Although the medieval distinctions between fair and unfair war did not outlaw an offensive or an aggression as such, "the present theory of war," writes Schmitt, introduces a kind of "*crime de l'attaque*": "Whoever fires the first shot or engages in any equivalent action is the 'felon' in this new criminal offense" (122), independent of any consideration of the just or unjust nature of the cause. For Schmitt, proof of this can be found in the Geneva Protocol of October 2, 1924, which, before ultimately being rejected by England, proposed an "outlawry of aggressive war" (269) and in the 1928 Kellogg-Briand pact with its "condemnation of war" (280).

From this point on, as Schmitt constantly emphasizes, war is transformed into a "police action" (*Polizeiaktion*) (299) of planetary dimensions against the danger of a generalized "global civil war."[40] This is thus a war without a *front*, where the enemy is not clearly localizable, a war that loses its traditional status as a war, as well as the international law that gave it its framework, to cede its place to terrorism and counterterrorism, to guerrilla tactics and other forms of diffuse struggle. This is, in Schmitt's eyes, the outcome and consequence of humanitarian pacifism when it causes the very existence of the political as such to tremble, for, on the one hand, "world peace" can be equivalent only to "complete and final depoliticalization" (*Concept*, 54), and, on the other, "humanity is not a political concept" (55). Connected through their reference to each other, humanity and peace, these two words that the first men to land on the moon wanted conjointly to inscribe—wanted to leave there in the form of an ineffaceable mark, at the border of what they thought was the new new world—these two notions seem destined also to signify, at the confines of known space, the end of politics.

This is the way we can understand a sentence that comes several times under Schmitt's plume as a way to mark a kind of ultimate limit, a *terminus ad quem*: "Humanity as such cannot wage war because it has no enemy, at least not on this planet."[41]

)) ((

For us Earthlings who read Schmitt a quarter of a century after his death, this same sentence might well become a *terminus a quo*, a point of departure.

What does this mean?

It is of course possible to understand Schmitt's formulation as announcing an enemy yet to come from the extraplanetary space that surrounds us.[42] Or better yet: as configuring the extraterrestrial cosmos as a place where the *possibility* of an opposition between friend and enemy subsists, in other words *the possibility of politics as such*, in its Schmittean understanding.

Let's be clear about this: It is obviously not a question of suggesting that politics, that any political action or agency has disappeared from planet Earth only to survive in the cosmos. This would be absurd, and every earthly minute dramatically testifies to the contrary. What must, however, be thought through is that a certain notion of politics, delimited in Schmitt's eyes by that to which it is opposed and that from which it is distinguished—by which he means, pell-mell, economics, ethics, aesthetics, and so on—has certainly deserted our globe, whatever those who cling to it may say.[43]

But if *the* political, as such, seems, therefore, more and more impossible to find or to present on Earth, we will not find it any better in an extraterrestrial space occupied in advance by humanity. Not only because, *out there just as much as right here*, the humanitarianism between humans accompanies the dissolution of the political into the police, that is, in the surveillance and maintenance of economic order (one can already begin to see what cosmic *industry appropriations* might be—in other words, the extension of the earthly market with its forced free circulation so as to exploit resources on other planets). But also and above all because the eventual adversaries of humanity, those extraterrestrials Kant will soon help us encounter in an entirely different way, could not be inscribed in the "friend-enemy polarity" that founds, for Schmitt, the pure concept of the political. Far from "disclos[ing] the possibility [of] the distinction of friend and enemy" (*Concept*, 35), a war against the *other* of humanity—against the *alien*, that other that is neither animal nor divine—this kind of war would seem rather to annihilate it. Bringing conflict "beyond the political" (as Schmitt puts it when he speaks of military operations that, already on Earth, are waged in the name of humanitarianism and are always presented as the last resort of a "definitively final war of humanity"), it would become the "absolute enemy" that, at the end of the *Theory of the Partisan*, replaces the "real enemy."[44]

Unless—another possibility, another eventuality—the *alien* were subject to measures that, underneath or beyond the political (which may come down to the same thing), would be of a *sanitary* nature. As a matter of fact, even as science fiction has been able to classically represent the intergalactic field as a space for battle in a fully and Schmitteanly political sense of the term (for example, in the double trilogy of *Star Wars*, George Lucas's space opera that began in 1977), science fiction also testifies to the perverse logic of humanitarianism extended to the treatment of *aliens*. Thus, *District 9* by Neill Blomkamp (2009) stages extraterrestrials whose spaceship is broken down above Johannesburg and whose troubling presence—people fear contamination—is managed by a multinational company charged with the task of isolating them in camps for cosmic refugees. Yet even before Ridley Scott's well-known *Alien* (1979), the paradigm of extraterrestrial viral virulence is already firmly installed in movies like *Invasion of the Body Snatchers* (directed by Don Siegel in 1956) where spores from outer space invade Earth and reproduce.

We will return with a Kantian gaze to certain figurations given to invaders that threaten humanity. Yet in our recent and very earthly legal history, we could already glean signs of their impolitic nature and of a *medicalization* of the cosmic threat.[45] Signs for this could be found for example in laws dealing with the earthly welcome we should reserve if not for extraterrestrials, then at least for those among us who might have been in contact with them. And these laws actually have nothing political about them; to the contrary, they make provisions for their treatment in terms of *public hygiene*. Those who return from *out there*, those who have had traffic with a dangerous elsewhere and have brushed up against its eventual inhabitants, whatever they may be (bacteria or higher organisms), are submitted to a *quarantine* that relegates them to an outside that is an enclave here on our earthly territory. On American soil, a law was thus passed in 1969 (and not abolished until 1991) that was imagined as a way of avoiding the dangers of contamination that astronauts might have posed after being "exposed" to extraterrestrial bodies. This federal law, baptized the Extraterrestrial Exposure Law, is what kept the members of the *Apollo 11* mission in isolation for twenty-one days after their return to planet Earth because of the fear that they may have been "touched directly" or that they might have "been in close proximity to . . . any person, property, animal or other form of life or matter who or which has been extra-terrestrially exposed."[46] Yet already in 1967, the UN's Outer Space Treaty, parts of which we have read, also included several similar precautions, such as those in its ninth article:

> States Parties to the Treaty shall pursue studies of outer space, including the Moon and other celestial bodies, and conduct exploration of them so as to avoid their harmful contamination and also adverse changes in the environment of the Earth resulting from the introduction of extraterrestrial matter.

Those who come back from the cosmos (those returnees staged in a series such as *The 4400* created by Scott Peters and broadcast starting in 2004) may well be human Earthlings like us all, but they still pose a potential threat that justifies their medical isolation. Those who were able to meet forms of extraterrestrial life are reduced to the status of a mere sanitary hazard, incarnating by metonymy—through contact and proximity—the hygienizing depoliticalization of the alien's alterity.[47]

We may thus doubt whether the extra-earthling enemy can be an enemy in Schmitt's sense of the term, in other words, in a *fully* political sense that implies its *presentability* in a warfaring confrontation. This is so much the case that Schmitt could have just as easily avoided giving the circumstances for his claim; he could have reduced it to its simplest form: Humanity, he could have written, *humanity as such does not and will not have an enemy.*

Neither on this planet, nor anywhere else.

)) ((

Every time I go up to the border of the United States, while I wait in line to get a visa, I recall these cosmic stakes without knowing whether or not they should make me smile. I remember them when, on the forms I have to fill out, I read the word that describes me as someone staking a claim to hospitality: *alien*, they say, I am a *nonresident alien*.[48] And it's while I allowed that word to resonate within me that I recently had an unforgettable conversation with a limousine driver who had come to pick me up after my arrival in Newark: all the way to Princeton, we spoke, pell-mell, about immigration problems, about my book project about extraterrestrials—he told me that he had seen them, or had at least indirectly met them over the course of one of his night fares—and, more generally, about questions of comparative politics between Sarkozy's France and Bush's America. For me, in spite of many overly obvious disagreements, this was a great moment of cosmopolitology, in the middle of the snow-covered landscapes of New Jersey.

But enough nostalgia, let us return to Schmitt.

Why is it that the affirmation that holds that humanity has no enemy is for us a *terminus a quo*, a starting point?

As we've just seen, what is at stake is not the arrival of an enemy worthy of the name from the cosmos. It's rather the *cosmopolitical* crisis of the very opposition between friend and enemy, as well as the possibility of their co-appearance, *in presence*, in a space—earthly or not—that can be defined as the theater of operations for an authentic war. And hence, what in effect opens up *from* Schmitt's sentence is the idea that humanity, to be thought as such *politically*, must be thought *at its very limit*, there where its constitutive enemy appears while disappearing: there where there are *no more* enemies that can be presented as such, that is to say, there where there are *more* enemies, *ever more*, in such a *surplus* of enmity that the cosmopolitical police, beyond or beneath politics, can only work toward their annihilation.

Humanity, and we'll return to this shortly with Kant, must be thought from the perspective of its other, from its outside, quite precisely there where this outside has not yet been given a figure or a face, since it is deprived of all our possible figurations. In short, humanity must be thought on the basis of the *wholly other* whose radical alterity cannot be localized in a circumscribed outside.

Beyond its simple factual dimension, this is how we might understand the group of legal events that have transformed the cosmos into a space that is *preoccupied* by humanity: on the one hand, because this cosmic space quite precisely does not house a merely *external* alterity that could be relegated to an outside from which humanity is absent (it is a fact that humanity authorizes itself to occupy it in advance), and on the other, because it is the cosmos that, with the *aliens* that might populate it, *is preoccupied with* humanity. It is the cosmos that, so to speak, has its heart set on defining humanity. The cosmos takes on the task of understanding humanity.

But if this outside is not a mere exteriority, if it does not have a pure delimitation, it therefore can also not be the space for a future—for a "pure future," as Schmitt wrote—that could be contrasted with a simple past or present. This is so much the case that we will perhaps be led to imagine, for example with Kant, a scenario that science fiction certainly anticipated: *They are already here.*

They—the others, the wholly other *aliens*—may well have already arrived and be among us, as so many productions for the screen have already suggested, and especially the famous series *The Invaders* (created by Larry Cohen and broadcast starting in 1967). Or as so many convinced ufologists have long thought, convinced as they are that (starting at the latest with the Roswell affair), we are not being told everything.[49]

In short, and without entering into the details of countless conspiracy and disinformation theories that thrive whenever one starts to think about extraterrestrials, what we now need to think through with the greatest philosophical rigor is that *they will have always already been here.*

This is what we are now going to attempt to do with Kant—by reading and rereading several major Kantian texts—alongside a few less well known others sometimes considered minor, where many surprises await us. But, before returning from the future to the past, from Schmitt's prophecies to Kant's auguries, a few final remarks are needed to help us prepare for takeoff and raising the anchor.

We mustn't forget the fact that in *Nomos of the Earth*, Schmitt cites Kant several times quite precisely to justify and lend support to his attachment to the value of presence and its telluric foundation. He first cites—in a loose way—the "Metaphysical First Principles of the Doctrine of Right" as a way of anchoring any possibility of possession into earth and to the Earth since land is the "main condition for the possibility of ownership and all further law, public as well as private."[50] It is thus as if for Schmitt, the telluric anchoring of his notion of *nomos* also went through Kant, strengthened its anchoring with a Kantian tie, for as Schmitt insists in the introductory pages to *Nomos of the Earth*:

Kant says: "First acquisition of a thing can be only acquisition of land." This "law of mine and thine that distributes the land to each man," [*austeilende Gesetz des Mein und Dein eines jeden am Boden*], as he puts it, is not positive law in the sense of later state codifications, or of the system legality in subsequent state constitutions; it is, and remains, the real core of a wholly concrete, historical, and political event: a land appropriation [*der wirkliche Kern eines ganz konkreten, geschichtlichen und politischen Ereignisses, nämlich der Landnahme*]. (48)

Schmitt thus cites Kant once again,[51] as if the better to tighten the knot that ties the foundation of right to the earth and to the Earth, to harness it to that founding event that is the *appropriation* of terrains and territories. Yet even though he takes fragments from Kant's text, he omits citing the movement in which these phrases are inscribed: the Kantian idea that "all men are originally in *common possession* of the land of the entire earth." In other words, quite simply, the legal notion of a *res communis humanitatis* that, as we have seen, is so important for the recent history of the appropriation or *preoccupation* of the cosmos.[52]

It's certainly not mere chance if Schmitt cloaks this context in silence, for as much as he seems to want to mobilize a Kantian tradition when it allows him to consolidate the earthly and earthbound anchoring for every legal apparatus, he also explicitly distances himself from Kant, as we would expect, when he accuses him of "total confusion" (*völliger Verwirrung*) on the subject of the notion of the "just enemy" (*das gerechten Feindes*) (Schmitt, *Nomos*, 169). If Kant plays such a contradictory role in the explanation of Schmittean *nomos*, if he intervenes to blur in advance the clear and precise definition of the enemy that founds the purity of the political, this indicates that we certainly need to turn to him in order to undo the grip of the metaphysical oppositions that, even as they allow Schmitt to produce one of the strongest and most lucid diagnoses of our current geopolitical situation— on the globalization we are now experiencing *at its limits*—prevent him from taking the path toward a truly cosmopolitical problematic: the path of the inhabitants of the cosmos.

When he deals with the question of the just enemy, Schmitt cites Kant's *Doctrine of Right* once again in a truncated and lapidary way, as if he wanted to stop and freeze it in the contradictions that remain incomprehensible without the movement that carries them: "A just enemy would be the one that I would be doing wrong by resisting; but then he would also not be my enemy," writes Kant (§60); and Schmitt can ironize all he wants by adding that "it would be difficult to misunderstand the concept of a just enemy any more seriously than Kant did." Yet in Kant's text, what immediately follows these words is a paragraph (§61) that introduces the question of perpetual peace, which, for as much as it is "an unachievable idea," nonetheless leads to bring states together within "a universal association of states" (*allgemeinen Staatenverein*), also described as "permanent congress" (*permanenten Staatencongress*), which leads without delay to the third and final section of *Public Right* (§62) devoted to "cosmopolitan right."

Schmitt barely mentions this cosmopolitan politics, except in a brief allusion to "the Hellenistic period": He says nothing about Kant's take on cosmopolitanism, neither here or elsewhere.[53] Of course, we know that Kant did not invent the word *cosmopolitanism*. As we can read in Diogenes Laërtius's *Lives and Opinions of Eminent Philosophers* (6:63), already in the fourth century B.C., Diogenes of Sinope (also known as Diogenes the Cynic) defined himself as *kosmopolitês*, "citizen of the world." This statement was often later attributed to Socrates, as Montaigne did: "When they asked Socrates where he came from he did not say 'From Athens,' but 'From the world.' He, whose thoughts were fuller and wider, embraced the universal world as his City."[54]

If the idea of the citizen of the world is therefore not Kantian, it is nonetheless Kant who gives it its modern articulation by inscribing it into the political horizon of world peace and imagining the institution of a League of Nations that could work toward realizing it in the future. In a way that is ambivalent and indirect, to say the least, Schmitt, in *Nomos of the Earth*, reluctantly recognizes this despite all by deeming Kantian cosmopolitanism, without naming it as such, a "success" that is all the greater given that it is deferred. "Immanuel Kant's philosophy, which brought the 18th century to a close, had an essentially different sort of influence on areas of international law, which became evident only in the 20th century" (168), he writes just before adding, at the very moment he is accusing the philosopher of having seriously misunderstood the concept of the "just enemy": "Perhaps this misunderstanding [*Verkennung*] already announces the normative abolition of interstate, European international law." A bit later on, Schmitt will deal with this "dissolution" or "decline" of the *jus publicum europaeum* in favor of a "general universal," of an "indistinctly universal international law" which, as we have seen, in his perspective destroys "the existing global order of the Earth." He continues, "But perhaps it is also a presentiment of a new *nomos* of the earth [*die Ahnung eines neuen Nomos der Erde*]" (168, translation slightly modified).

This attributes a great deal of importance and credit to what was earlier qualified as mere confusion (*Verwirrung*). It so happens that in the very last pages of his book, when Schmitt considers what he calls "the problem of the new *nomos* of the earth"—a problem he will leave wide open and gaping with an enormous question mark—he returns to the idea of the just enemy, of the *justus hostis*, which is legally recognized.[55] And if he does so, it is, as you will remember, to announce its disappearance in favor of a transformation of war "into a police action against troublemakers [*Störenfriede*, lit. those who disturb the peace], criminals [*Verbrecher*], and pests [*Schädlinge*, lit. parasites, harmful insects]" (*Nomos*, 321).

It is thus as if, from Schmitt's perspective, and without his full avowal, Kant perhaps anticipated a space beyond the political, or at least *this* political that was founded on the purity of the friend-enemy opposition and on "the mutual concept of war conceived in terms of an equal plane" (*auf gleicher Ebene gedachte gegenseitige Kriegsbegriff*). If the horizon or horizontality, if the *grounds* for this concept are lacking, then it is probably no longer on our telluric star that the question of a new *nomos* must be posed.

In short, we need to wonder whether or not humanity is ready to raise the anchor on this spaceship that, according to Schmitt himself, "the planet we inhabit, . . . the Earth itself" has become.

Unless perhaps humanity has *already done so*? Unless we—we humans, we Earthlings—have *always already* cast off?

CHAPTER 2

Kant in the Land of Extraterrestrials

Kant, like many philosophers before him, believed in the existence of intelligent extraterrestrial life, in a form of life superior to the one known to us as humans on the Earth. Starting with one of his first pieces of writing (*Universal Natural History and Theory of the Heavens,* written in 1755 when he was twenty-one years old) all the way through one of the last (*Anthropology from a Pragmatic Point of View,* published in 1798, six years before his death), Kant, apparently without making it a major theme of his philosophy, will have regularly summoned inhabitants of other planets, inviting them over and over again into his discourse.

Why Not? Philosofiction of the Wholly Other

In the third part of his *Theory of the Heavens,* Kant thus declares: "I am of the opinion that it is just not necessary to assert that all planets must be inhabited. even though it would be nonsense to deny this in regard to all or even only most of them."[1] For Kant this is, according to the word he uses, a "conjecture"; without affirming or denying it, the philosopher asks: *Why* would there *not* be forms of intelligent or reasonable life (life endowed with reason) elsewhere than on Earth?

Why not? was also the question that set the fundamental tone for Fontenelle's famous *Conversations on the Plurality of Worlds*[2] (whose first edition appeared in 1686, in other words almost sixty years before Kant's *Theory of the Heavens*).[3] It was indeed a movement of enthusiasm in the form of a *why not?* that draws the narrator of Fontenelle's dialogue into a kind of enthusiasm for universal cosmic population as he speaks with the marquise, his somewhat skeptical interlocutor:

> "The Moon, according to all appearances, is inhabited; why won't Venus be too?"
>
> "But," the Marquise interrupted, "always by saying 'Why not?' are you going to put people on all the planets for me?"
>
> "Don't doubt it," I replied. "This 'Why not' has a power which allows it to populate everything."[4]

Why not indeed?

The question demands our complete attention: What is marked and found in the guise of this negative interrogation is the space of a *fiction* that not only dictates the gracious and light-hearted tone of texts such as these *Conversations* but is also what comes to haunt even the most formally rigorous philosophical works, as we will see with the *Critique of the Power of Judgment* and other writings by Kant. This space is the element of what I will be calling *philosofiction* (as one speaks of science fiction).[5]

)) ((

In the last work that Kant, using notes taken by auditors of his course, wrote and published while he was alive, his *Anthropology from a Pragmatic Point of View,* the philosofictive question of extraterrestrial life returns in a gripping and insistent way. The second part, devoted to "Anthropological Characteristic," in other words, to the "way of cognizing the interior of the human being from the exterior," deals successively with the character of the "person," of the "sexes," of the "peoples," and of the "races," and concludes with the "character of the species." When it comes down to this last category, Kant more or less admits that anthropology is powerless as a discourse on the human: How could we, he basically says, know what characterizes the human species in its specificity, in other words, what differentiates it from other species, if these other species remain inaccessible to our experience and unknowable? Kant declares that the "*terrestrial* rational being" is thus impossible to characterize and condemned to remain undefined or undetermined:

> We shall not be able to name its character because we have no knowledge of the *non-terrestrial* beings that would enable us to indicate their characteristic property and so to characterize this terrestrial being among rational beings in general. It seems, therefore, that the problem of indicating the character of the human species is absolutely insoluble, because the solution would have to be made through experience by means of the comparison of two *species* of rational being, but experience does not offer us this possibility.[6]

Earthlings are incomparable in the absence of an experience or possible knowledge of extraterrestrial life. And yet while they would like to think of themselves as rational beings, these same Earthlings, Kant foremost among them, continue to appeal to a term of comparison, however unpresentable it may be.

Without a comparative characterization, one that Kant's anthropology seems grudgingly to abandon, Kant at first appears to resign himself to defining "the character of the species" intrinsically, in other words without leaving the Earth and accepting the necessity of staying here, and of staying here *together*:

> The character of the species, as it is known from the experience of all ages and by all peoples, is this: that taken collectively (the human race as one whole), it is a multitude of persons, existing successively and side by side, who *cannot do* without being together peacefully and yet cannot *avoid*

constantly being objectionable to one another. Consequently, they feel destined by nature to develop . . . into a *cosmopolitan society* (*cosmopolitismus*) that is constantly threatened by disunion but generally progresses toward a coalition.[7]

These cosmopolitans, the citizens of the cosmos that we are, will thus remain Earthlings, condemned to sharing the Earth among ourselves. And it is also on the Earth that we will have to deal with the question as to whether the human species, impossible to characterize in any way other than as a mass of Earthlings condemned to coexisting with one another, "is to be regarded as a good or bad race" (*Anthropology*, 237).

If Kant thus seems determined to judge the Earthlings that we are in an *intraterrestrial* way, this is nonetheless a problem for him. It's almost as if he *cannot* entirely abandon the *extraterrestrial* comparison, even though he has just called it impossible. Already, when he speaks of the human species as a "race," he is structurally bound to position it in its relation to another, even if that other is unknown: "the human species," he writes, "which, when one thinks of it as a species of rational *beings on earth* in comparison with rational beings on other planets" (237). The comparison, which it was necessary to dismiss several pages before, thus almost immediately returns. It comes back, against all odds: Extraterrestrials just keep on coming back and will continue to do so.

These inhabitants of other worlds land one last time in Kant's *Anthropology* when it concludes with a consideration of "the moral physiognomy of our species" (237). Kant writes, in what are almost the concluding words:

It is already clear enough from the concealment of a good part of one's thoughts, which every human being finds necessary, that in our race everyone finds it advisable to be on his guard and not to allow others to view *completely* how he is. This already betrays the propensity of our species to be evil-minded toward one another.

It could well be that on some other planet there might be rational beings who could not think in any other way but aloud; that is, they could not have any thoughts that they did not at the same time *utter,* whether awake or dreaming, in the company of others or alone. What kind of behavior toward others would this produce, and how would it differ from that of our human species? (237)

In the last pages of the last work written by Kant, the philosopher's effort to characterize Earthlings seems decidedly unable to do without the only cosmopolitans worthy of the name: inhabitants of the cosmos who are thus destined to return over and over again whenever one considers the human species *from a certain point of view.*

)) ((

Did Kant truly believe in extraterrestrials? Did he believe in them in the same way that some today say they have witnessed signs that have purportedly come to announce the arrival of inhabitants come from other worlds?

Kant did indeed consign his convictions here and there in his writing.[8] And one can also find passages under his signature which, if distractedly read, might resemble the hook for a science-fiction screenplay from today—for example, this one from the *Critique of the Power of Judgment*:

If someone were to perceive a geometrical figure, for instance a regular hexagon, drawn in the sand in an apparently uninhabited land, . . . he would not be able to judge as a ground of the possibility of such a shape the sand, the nearby sea, the wind, the footprints of any known animals, or any other nonrational cause. (242)

Reading this paragraph, one might think, for example, of Night Shyamalan's 2003 film *Signs,* where the arrival of extraterrestrials is first announced by immense geometrical figures cut out of the fields in a sparsely inhabited region of the United States (Bucks County, Pennsylvania). Just as Kant, when faced with the hypothetical regular hexagon drawn in the desert, affirms that "no natural cause in nature . . . can contain the causality for such an effect," in other words that in this case one finds the result of "a concept that can be given only by reason," so do Shyamalan's characters repeatedly dismiss one by one the possible natural causes for the improbable drawings they discover traced on a large scale in the cornfields: The children of Graham Hess (Mel Gibson), his daughter Bo and his son Morgan, awakened early in the morning by the barking of dogs, immediately think that "God did it," something their father refuses to believe; and yet, speaking with the representative of the local police he has just called in, he himself says that "it can't be by hand, it's too perfect." The hypothesis of a criminal act is thus dismissed. And the suspicion of an extraterrestrial cause becomes insistent when the television broadcasts similar images from all over the world of giant signs engraved into cornfields, crop signs from all over the Earth.

But beyond this kind of superficial analogy between Kant and contemporary science fiction,[9] and beyond the declared opinions of the philosopher himself, what awaits us is a much more radical question: We will not be trying to figure out what Kant really believed deep down about the existence of extraterrestrial life; instead, we will attempt to outline the necessity of a *why not?*, of a philosofictive dimension from which philosophy cannot escape and to which it must be exposed whenever it seeks to judge and to think about judgment. Better yet, whenever it is confronted with what is called a *point of view*.

)) ((

The narrator of Fontanelle's *Conversations on the Plurality of Worlds* explicitly announced that there will be "communication between the Earth and the Moon" (34); to a still incredulous marquise he maintained that "someday we'll go to the Moon" (34).

In the conclusion to his *Theory of the Heavens*, Kant imagined in a more prudently conjectural way if not exactly a future epoch for interstellar journeys,[10] then at least the possibility of staying in other worlds after death.

> Should the immortal soul remain forever attached to this point in space, to our Earth for the whole infinity of its future duration, which is not interrupted by the grave itself, but only changed? . . . Who knows whether it is not intended to get to know at close quarters those distant spheres of the solar system? . . . Perhaps some further spheres of the planetary system will form around them in order to prepare new places for us to reside in other heavens, after the completed passage of time prescribed for our stay here. (*Theory of the Heavens*, 307)

Who knows, really?

And why not?

And what surprises would then await interplanetary explorations, either while we're alive or once we're buried? What forms of life might we encounter to which a human species might finally become comparable?

If, in his writings after the critical turn, Kant will stop himself (with a certain amount of difficulty) from full-fledged free comparative speculation on the inhabitants of different worlds,[11] here, in this "precritical" text, he launches into a reasoned attempt to classify extraterrestrial ways of existing and thinking:

> It must be far lighter and more volatile matters that constitute the body of an inhabitant of Jupiter so that the slight stirring with which the Sun can act at this distance, can move these machines just as powerfully as it does in the lower regions, and so that I can summarize everything in one general concept: *The material of which the inhabitants of different planets . . . are*

formed must . . . be of a lighter and finer type . . . the further they are away from the sun. . . . The . . . liveliness of the concepts they receive through external impressions, along with the faculty to put them together, and finally also the agility in the actual exercise, in short, the entire extent of their perfection stands under a certain rule, according to which they become more and more excellent and perfect in proportion to the distance of their domiciles from the Sun. . . . The perfection of the spiritual world as well as the material world increases and progresses in the planets from Mercury on to Saturn or perhaps even beyond it (insofar as there are yet other planets), in a correct sequence of degrees in proportion to their distances from the Sun. (Theory of the Heavens, 300–2)

In this free and limitless ethnocosmological speculation, Kant does not yet seem overly concerned with critically regulating the fictional dimension inherent in his philosophy. Despite the warning he places at the beginning of this third part of his *Theory of the Heavens* ("I am of the view that it would be a dishonor to the character of philosophy if one were to use it to maintain, in a kind of thoughtlessness, free excesses of wit with some apparent truth, even if one were to declare that this were merely an amusement" [295]), what gets him carried away is what he himself named "the freedom to invent" (295). And it carries him away to the advantage of a pleasure that, as his conclusion hints, seems to be aesthetic in nature:

It is permissible, it is proper to amuse oneself with such ideas. . . . Indeed, once one has filled one's mind with such observations . . . the view of the starry sky on a clear night gives one a kind of pleasure that only noble souls feel. In the universal stillness of nature and the calmness of the senses the immortal spirit's hidden faculty of cognition speaks an ineffable language and provides undeveloped concepts that can certainly be felt but not described. (307)

These lines that come to close *Theory of the Heavens* are not without recalling in advance certain passages in *The Critique of the Power of Judgment*, to which we will return. But above all, the speculation acts as if—yes, *as if*—the geographic and temporal perspective of humanity's progress, a very Earthling perspective at any rate, were projected into the cosmos and stretched to cosmic space. For it is the Earthling and the Earth who, in the Kantian scale of living cosmic beings, are thus found *in the middle*, at the average or median point. This point is certainly no longer the center, as it was in the ancient cosmological systems before Newton or Copernicus, yet it nonetheless keeps several of its characteristics:

> Human nature, which in the scale of being holds, as it were, the middle rung, is . . . equidistant from both. If the idea of the most sublime classes of sensible creatures living on Jupiter or Saturn provokes the jealousy of human beings and discourages them with the knowledge of their own humble position, a glance at the lower stages brings content and calms them again. The beings on the planets Venus and Mercury are reduced far below the perfection of human nature. What a view worthy of our astonishment! on one side we saw thinking creatures among whom a Greenlander or a Hottentot would be a Newton; on the other side, we saw people who would admire Newton as if he were an ape. (*Theory of the Heavens*, 152)

What is important here is not really the simple cosmic expansion or amplification of a geocentric anthropology or geography that posits a correspondence between Newton's Europe and Jupiter, primitive ethnic groups and Mercury. In this sense, the extraterrestrial fiction is not exactly the equivalent of Montesquieu's *Persian Letters*, or of any other recourse to the artifice of exoticism as a way, under the fictive cover of an *out there*, to speak of what is happening *down here*, at home. For the philosofiction of the *Theory of the Heavens*—which, as we will see, survives in attenuated forms in Kant's later writings—seems to have to necessarily take itself beyond possible experience: not simply toward the other, but rather toward the *wholly other*.[12]

)) ((

This anthropogeocentrism that secretly continues to regulate Kant's cosmologic discourse in spite of the constant references to the Newtonian system and the affirmation of the superiority of life on planets far from the Sun; the privilege accorded in spite of it all to Earth and its Earthlings at the precise moment that it's a question of leaving it can already be found in Fontenelle's work. In *Conversations on the Plurality of Worlds*, it is also European ethnocentrism that, stretched out to the dimensions of the universe, dictated the logic of the speculations about the characteristics of the inhabitants of other planets. This is what allows the marquise, when speaking of Venusians, closer to the Sun, to say: "They resemble our Moors of Grenada, a small, black people, sunburnt, full of verve and fire, always amorous, writing verses, loving music, inventing celebrations, dances, and tournaments every day" (49). And the narrator goes one step further:

> "Allow me to tell you," I replied, "that you don't know the Venusians very well. Compared to them our Moors would be like Lapps and Greenlanders for coldness and stupidity. But what about the inhabitants of Mercury? They're even closer to the Sun. They must be vivacious to the point of madness! I believe they have no memory, no more than most savages; that they never think deeply on anything; that they act at random and by sudden movements." (*Conversations*, 49)

As is the case in Kant's *Theory of the Heavens*, the solar system is here a kind of mirror of the ethnogeographic and racial characterizations that hold here on Earth. This is so much the case that, in these cosmic and often comic philosofictions (one is tempted to laugh at such sidereal and siderated racism),[13] it seems that we are seeing a double movement: On the one hand, as we just read, the extraterrestrial, however outlying he may be, could not be given figure or fiction with no tie whatsoever to earthly anthropology; but on the other hand, as we have glimpsed, Earthlings cannot see themselves *as such*, as a reasonable species or race within the universe, unless they detach themselves from their planetary ground and base as a way of being transported, at least in their imagination, toward the point of view of the wholly other.

Points of View (From the Deserted Island to the Universe)

Even for a merely exterior or distant gaze or glance, the question of the *point of view* appears omnipresent and is posed pretty much everywhere in Kant's work. One can already hear it in the indications most visible to the naked eye, in the titles: *Anthropology from a Pragmatic Point of View,* "Idea for a Universal History from a Cosmopolitan Perspective," for example. And once you look a bit more closely than the titles, you notice that it is constantly evoked and thematized in the texts.

Two examples, among many others.

In the introduction to the 1793 treatise (lengthily) titled *On the Old Saw: That May Be Right in Theory But It Won't Work in Practice*, one reads:

> The philosophically scandalous pretense is not infrequently advanced—that what may be true in it is still invalid in practice. And this pretense is advanced in a tone of lofty disdain full of presumption to have reason itself reformed by experience in the area which reason deems its highest honor, and with the sapient conceit to see farther and more clearly with the eyes of a mole, fixed upon experience, than with the eyes of a being that was made to stand erect and to behold the heavens.[14]

Between experience and reason, it's therefore a question of perspective, of how one looks at things: The shortsightedness of experience contrasts with the far-sightedness of reason, which turns toward celestial regions and the cosmos.

A certain refusal of experience's shortsightedness is also marked in a passage from the second part of *The Conflict of the Faculties*, where the progress of the human species is at stake:

> Even if we felt that the human race, considered as a whole, was to be conceived as progressing and proceeding forward for however long a time, still no one can guarantee that now, this very moment, with regard to the physical disposition of our species, the epoch of its decline would not be liable to occur; and inversely, if it is moving backwards, and in an accelerated fall into baseness, a person may not despair even then of encountering a juncture . . . where the moral predisposition of our race would be able to turn anew toward the better. . . . If the course of human affairs seems so senseless to us, perhaps it lies in a poor choice of position from which we regard it. Viewed from the earth, the planets sometimes move backwards, sometimes forward, and sometimes not at all. But if the standpoint selected is the sun, an act which only reason can perform, according to the Copernican hypothesis they move constantly in their regular course.[15]

Kant thus seems to suggest that in order to judge the course of earthly affairs, there is a point of view that would make them appear regular instead of chaotic. And this point of view, which would be that of reason beyond experience, is described by an astronomical or cosmological analogy: as if it were a question of adopting Copernicus's heliocentric perspective in order to understand humanity's course.

As if, yes, and *only as if*, for Kant immediately continues:

> But, and this is precisely the misfortune, we are not capable of placing ourselves in this position when it is a question of the prediction of free actions. For that would be the standpoint of Providence which is situated beyond all human wisdom, and

which likewise extends to the free actions of the human being; these actions, of course, the human being can *see*, but not *fore-see* with certitude. (*Conflict of the Faculties*, 300)

At the very moment he appeals to a superior point of view that he describes in cosmological terms, and even though by naming Copernicus, he summons a perspective unhooked from all geo-centrism as being the only one that can analogically characterize the gaze required to judge earthly affairs, Kant, with the very same gesture, prohibits it.

As it stands, here too, here and elsewhere, Kant seems to need the extra-earthly philosofiction in order to be able to think or judge the humanity of the human species and the eventual prog-ress of humanity in turn; but, at the same time, he knows and de-clares it to be impossible or untenable.

In short, *the necessary philosofiction is the one there is not.*

)) ((

But let us return to Earth for a moment, back to Earthlings. Because the necessity of adopting the point of view of the other, perhaps of the wholly other, also starts down here, as Kant's *Anthropology* shows.

Kant, who never in his whole life left his native Königsberg, does indeed wonder, in the preface, just after having announced that he will be looking for "knowledge of the human being as a *citizen of the world*," how he might extend the anthropological point of view to "other men."[16] And his answer is double: On the one hand, he says, fictions and fictive travel will be used; but on the other hand, a priori knowledge will be needed, knowledge that one will have to acquire at home before going somewhere else in imagination. For the philosofictive traveler, this is how the world will be able to grow:

Travel belongs to the means of broadening the range of anthropology, even if it is only the reading of travel books. But if one wants to know what to look for abroad, in order to broaden the range of anthropology, first one must have acquired knowledge of human beings at home, through social intercourse with one's townsmen or countrymen. Without such a plan (which already presupposes knowledge of human beings) the citizen of the world remains very limited with regard to anthropology. . . . While not exactly sources for anthropology, there are nevertheless aids: world history, biographies, even plays and novels. For although the latter two are not actually based on experience and truth, but only on invention, and while here the exaggeration of characters and situations in which beings are placed is allowed, as if in a dream, thus appearing to show us nothing concerning knowledge of human beings—yet even so . . . while they are exaggerated in degree, they must nevertheless correspond to human nature in kind. (Kant, *Anthropology*, 4–5)

If it is true that the search for impartial judgment was Kant's great affair—he who kept wanting to think the faculty of judgment as the adoption of the point of view of the other, even every other as being each time the wholly other[17]—it is probably for this very reason that he found himself confronted with the question of the *as if,* of fiction or of fictionality, as the only possible access to this expanded horizon. Kant, as Hannah Arendt has reminded us, was "an eager reader of all sorts of travel reports" (Arendt, *Kant's Political Philosophy*, 44). And, she added, "he—who never left Königsberg—knew his way around in both London and Italy." If we believe Arendt, it is "precisely because he wanted to know so much about so many countries" that Kant, in the end, "had no time to travel." Having thus chosen to travel through the mediation of fiction or of accounts, because of the very cosmopolitanism that pushed him toward *all other* citizens of the world, Kant seemed destined to philosofiction, as both an opening and a limit—as an imaginary access to the other, but without experience of the other.

It will therefore come as no surprise if, even in the most rigorously philosophical works, the ones that, like the *Critique of the Power of Judgment*, are thus apparently the least marred by fiction, one of the commonplaces of travel literature appears several times: what Kant himself calls "Robinsonades" (157).

The Robinsonian theme of the deserted island does indeed appear several times in the Third Critique (which dates from 1790). And it already appears almost at the beginning, in the famous and important paragraph (§2) that defines the judgment of taste bearing on the beautiful as disinterested:

> The satisfaction that we combine with the representation of the existence of an object is called interest. . . . But if the question is whether something is beautiful, one does not want to know whether there is anything that is or that could be at stake, for us or for someone else, in the existence of the thing, but rather how we judge it in mere contemplation. . . . If someone asks me whether I find the palace that I see before me beautiful, I may well say . . . like the Iroquois sachem, that nothing in Paris pleased him better than the cook-shops; or else . . . if I were to find myself on an uninhabited island, without any hope of ever coming upon human beings again, and could conjure up such a magnificent structure through my mere wish, I would not even take the trouble of doing so if I had already had a hut that was comfortable enough for me. . . . But that is not what is at issue here. One only wants to know whether the mere representation of the object is accompanied with satisfaction in me, however indifferent I might be with regard to the existence of the object of this representation. . . . Everyone must admit that a judgment about beauty in which there is mixed the least interest is very partial and not a pure judgment of taste. (Kant, *Critique of the Power of Judgment*, 90–91)

Before he is able to declare the judgment of taste disinterested, Kant seems here to hope briefly to go through the diverse anthropological forms of interest or desire by tracing out a widening or increasing abstraction of the point of view: the exotic point of view of the sachem (which he actually borrows from a travel story)[18] and the fictive one of a hypothetical Robinson, isolated from humanity. From the one to the other, from the sachem to Robinson, there is progress toward the universal: If the sachem is supposed to make us smile with the idiom of his slightly gluttonous taste, the man of the deserted island is already an approximation of humans in general, of humanity as such, independently of the context he finds himself in. This is universal man for, paradoxically, on his island he is isolated from any kind of particularism.

)) ((

The Robinsonian figure of the deserted island[19] returns in a later paragraph of the *Critique of the Power of Judgment* (§41) which in a way follows an inverse move. After having established, in effect, that a pure judgment of taste had to be independent of any interest for the object—that it had to be a kind of island where the faculty of judgment isolates itself or makes itself insular, as an aesthetic faculty, in relation to the faculty of desire (§§2–5)—Kant had put forth a first definition of the beautiful: "*Taste* is the faculty for judging an object or a kind of representation through a satisfaction or dissatisfaction *without any interest*. The object of such a satisfaction is called *beautiful*" (96). Once he has acquired this definition, Kant can look back. And it is once again the Robinsonade that allows him to concede that, *after the fact*, an empirical interest can come to be associated with pure aesthetic judgment:

> That the judgment of taste, by which something is declared to be beautiful, must have no interest *for its determining ground* has been adequately demonstrated above. But from that it does not follow that *after it has been given as a pure aesthetic judgment* [emphasis mine] no interest can be combined with

it. . . . The beautiful interests empirically only in *society*. . . .
For himself alone a human being abandoned on a desert island
would not adorn either his hut or himself, nor seek out or still
less plant flowers in order to decorate himself; rather, only in
society does it occur to him to be not merely a human being
but also, in his own way, a refined human being (the beginning
of civilization): for this is how we judge someone who is in-
clined to communicate his pleasure to others and is skilled at
it, and who is not content with an object if he cannot feel his
satisfaction in it in community with others. (*Critique of the
Power of Judgment*, §41, 176–77)

On his isolated island, Robinson thus cannot have a *cosmetic*
drive because his radical insularity cuts him off from any *cosmopolitical* perspective. The Robinsonian theme plays a double role.
On the one hand, when it is a matter of ensuring the disinterested
purity of a judgment of taste, it is the hinge, the pivot that allows
the man particularized by his context to pass over to humanity in
general, to the human being reduced by his or her insularity to the
pure humanity he or she naturally bears. And on the other hand,
once that purity has already been acquired, Robinson becomes the
fiction of a human incapable of putting an (overly) pure aesthetic
judgment into the service of a *superior* interest, in other words,
communicability, as the human characteristic par excellence.

In other words, the moment of the judgment of taste on
beauty, as pure, must indeed be Robinsonian; but it must also be
sociable, in other words, oriented by the perspective of its universal distribution [*partage*], with regards to which Robinson is very
much beneath the Iroquois. In terms of point of view, *from the
point of view of the point of view* adopted in the judgment of
taste, this judgment must be both absolutely singular (isolated,
insular on that island of singularity that the judging subject is)
and perfectly capable of becoming universal.

As you will have understood, Robinson is a moment within a
series that makes the point of view vary. He is a point on the line

of points of view that goes from the Iroquois sachem to Coperni-can reason, from Parisian cook-shops all the way to the sun. Yet, interrupting that line, Robinson is also no doubt a kind of extra-terrestrial on Earth: He is the necessary philosofiction, a philoso-fictive being necessary for thinking about certain characteristics of the human species by isolating them.

The Orient of Judgment

It is probably time now to get down to reading that Third Cri-tique, which, on the basis of the aesthetic experience, lays the groundwork for the expansion of the point of view of the judging subject to cosmopolitan dimensions.

It is time to read it as it must be read, starting at the beginning, in other words from the right angle and with the right perspec-tive, rather than being too far away or too close up and content-ing oneself with overly general allusions or diving into the details, as we have done up until now.

How should we orient ourselves, then, in the *Critique of the Power of Judgment*? How should we situate ourselves in relation to it so that our gaze can take it in? How can we get a bird's-eye view of it before breaking pathways into it that will allow us to track the virtual place of the wholly other? What directions should we take and toward which horizons?

These questions are not abusive metaphors when it comes down to orientation within the discourse signed in Kant's name. For it is Kant himself who, in a 1786 text, proposes an "extended concept . . . of orientation." In this essay called "What Is Orienta-tion in Thinking?" Kant writes, as if he were speaking of the antique astrolabes that predated our current GPS:

To *orient* oneself, in the proper sense of the word, means to use a given direction . . . in order to find the others, and in par-ticular that of the *sunrise*. If I see the sun in the sky and know that it is now midday, I know how to find south, west, north, and east. . . . I can extend this concept even further if I equate it with the ability to orient oneself not just in space, i.e. mathematically, but also in *thought*, i.e. *logically*. It is easy to guess by analogy that this will be the means whereby pure reason regulates its use when, taking leaving of known objects (of experience), it seeks to extend its sphere beyond the frontiers of experience.[20]

What Kant calls, a few pages later, the "signpost" or "compass" of thinking will thus be "a purely rational belief" that allows him to "orient himself on his rational wanderings in the field of supra-sensory objects" (Kant, *Political Writings*, 245).

In regard to this, one might wonder (and we will return to this) if the extraterrestrial hypotheses, these philosofictions, are not instruments for getting one's bearings: Like navigators' sextants, they serve to anchor the traveling observer's point of view *somewhere*.

)) ((

Yet as we were preparing to read, our question was: How can one orient oneself in the *Critique of the Power of Judgment*, in this work that, for the first time in the history of philosophy, intends to found the aesthetic domain in its autonomy, in other words, to make it into an isolated field, a kind of island?[21]

At the end of his introduction, Kant himself, as if to assist his navigator reader on the verge of undertaking his or her journey to a heretofore unknown territory, not only gives a map or a plan of his thinking's trajectory ("Division of the Entire Work," 83) but also a "table" of the faculties that situates the faculty of judgment in relation to understanding and reason in an "overview" (82).

It is with this panoramic glance, this shot [*saisie*] from above (a kind of overview effect), that we are supposed zoom in dizzyingly onto the veritable beginning at the moment when we are raising the anchor to sail away and read:

First Part
Critique of the Aesthetic Power of Judgment
First Section
Analytic of the Aesthetic Power of Judgment
First Book
Analytic of the Beautiful
First Moment
of the judgment of taste, concerning its quality
§1
The judgment of taste is aesthetic

Come from faraway to approach this new land, here we are
then at the threshold of this text, with the sensation of having
switched the bird's-eye view for a mole's eyes, ready to get lost in
the text's tunnels.

From up so close, what can we make out?

> In order to decide [*unterscheiden*] whether or not something is
> beautiful, we do not relate the representation by means of
> understanding to the object for cognition, but rather relate
> it . . . to the subject and its feeling of pleasure or displeasure.
> The judgment of taste is therefore not a cognitive judgment,
> hence not a logical one, but is rather aesthetic, by which is
> understood one whose determining ground cannot be *other
> than subjective.* (§1, 89)

Yet this subjective point of view that differentiates between a
judgment of taste and a cognitive judgment is also, as we have
seen, a disinterested point of view in which "one must not be in
the least biased in favor of the existence of the thing" (§2, 90). It
thus cannot be a question of the agreeable or of what is good—
perspectives that Kant carefully eliminates one by one (§§3–5).[22]

But it is precisely *because* the aesthetic point of view is *both
subjective and disinterested*—without "bias"—that it can and
even must make a claim to *universality.* This is not the objective

universality of cognitive judgment, but what Kant names, in an apparently paradoxical turn of phrase, the *subjective universality* of satisfaction felt when faced with the beautiful.

> For since it is not grounded in any inclination of the subject (nor in any other underlying interest), but rather the person making the judgment feels himself completely *free* with regard to the satisfaction that he devotes to the object, he cannot discover as grounds of the satisfaction any private conditions, pertaining to his subject alone, and must therefore regard it as grounded in those that he can also presuppose in everyone else [*jedem anderen*]; consequently he must believe himself to have grounds for expecting a similar pleasure of everyone [*jedermann*]. Hence he will speak of the beautiful as if beauty were a property of the object and the judgment logical (constituting a cognition of the object . . .), although it is only aesthetic . . . ; because it still has the similarity with logical judgment that its validity for everyone [*jedermann*] can be presupposed. . . . Consequently there must be attached to the judgment of taste, with the consciousness of an abstraction in it from all interest, a claim to validity for everyone [*jedermann*] without the universality that pertains to objects, i.e., it must be combined with a claim to subjective universality [*subjektive Allgemeinheit*]. (§6, 96–97)

Because my judgment is supposed to be untethered from everything that could anchor me to a particular context woven by the network of my interests, it could be everyone's. *As if,* but *only as if,* it were an objective judgment shared by all. Or more exactly by each and every one (Kant writes *jedermann* and not *alle*).

But who is this *each and every one* who, without any guarantee of any objectivity, seems included straightaway in my pure aesthetic point of view? And what does this insular purity of the aesthetic mean if *each one* thus straightaway virtually occupies the point of view of this one among others that I am?

Further on, in an important paragraph that still awaits our attention, Kant will name this point of view of the *jedermann*, of each one, the place or the site (*Stelle*) of "every other" (*jedes andern*). And while reading it, we will wonder, just how far does the opening of the aesthetic point of view extend in its inclusive broadening? In other words, what are these others that can respond to the distributivity implied in the adjective *each* or *every* (*jeder*)? To what extent are they other, perhaps wholly other?

)) ((

Let's begin again.

If the judgment of taste, as we have seen, is truly disinterested only when being formulated on a kind of deserted island, if every time it is Robinsonian because it has to be isolated from bias by a radical insularization, this pure aesthetic judgment may well resemble that of an extraterrestrial fallen to Earth: Faced with the object I call beautiful, and in order to be able to say it is such, I find myself adopting a point of view that not only *could* be, but that *should* be that of an inhabitant of another planet. In this sense, there is always something Martian—or Saturnine, of Venusian, etc.—in beauty. *As if* it weren't wholly earthly or terrestrial, but without needing to be divine.

But this Robinson, this extraterrestrial Earthling that I am, every time I judge beauty in an insular and disinterested isolation, is also oriented *by* or *toward* the universal point of view of each and every one.

By or *toward*? This is indeed the question Kant asks: Is it the satisfaction inspired by the beautiful object, he wonders, that precedes universal communicability, in order to then turn *toward* it? Or, on the contrary, is it universal communicability that, coming before the pleasure taken at the representation of the object, in a way provokes this pleasure as its effect and its consequence? Is judgment then oriented *by* universal communicability?

This problem is in fact "the key to the critique of taste" Kant specifies. So much so that it is thus "worthy of full attention," as he insists before resolutely deciding in favor of the second hypothesis:

> If the pleasure in the given object came first . . . such a procedure would be self-contradictory. For such a pleasure would be none other than mere agreeableness in sensation; and hence by its very nature could have only private validity. . . . Thus it is the universal capacity for the communication of the state of mind . . . which . . . must serve as the ground [of the judgment of taste] and have the pleasure in the object as a consequence. (§9, 102)

We will return to the content or structure of this state of mind (*Gemütszustand*) that, in aesthetic judgment, is universally communicable (literally shareable with, *mitteilbar, mitteilungsfähig*). For now, what is important is that this communicability comes *before* the pleasure (*Lust*) that thus seems *to result from it*.

Yet with whom does one virtually share this state of mind? To whom is it likely to be communicated or addressed in advance, even before and in order for it to please?[23]

To each and every one, Kant was saying (*jedermann*, §6); which thus also means, as he says further on, to each other, to each one who is other, to every other (*jedes andern*, §40). Kant suggests in effect that "one could even define taste as the faculty for judging that which makes our feeling in a given representation universally communicable" (§40, 175). And that in this sense, one could also give the faculty for judging the name or the nickname of "common sense" (*gemeinschaftlichen Sinnes*). This baptism is in fact the pretext for what Kant himself calls a "digression" over the course of which he enumerates three "maxims" that, if they do not strictly belong to the critique of taste, can nonetheless serve to elucidate its principles. The maxims "are the following: 1. To think for oneself [*Selbstdenken*]; 2. To think in the position of everyone else [*an der Stelle jedes andern*]; 3. Always to think in accord with oneself [*mit sich selbst einstimmig*]" (174). Framed by the two others that refer to the same, to oneself (*selbst*), the central maxim, the second one, is the only one of which Kant will say, at the end of his digression, that it is "that of the faculty of judging" (175). Whereas the first and last maxims are related to understanding and reason, this one, the one that properly concerns judgment, is related to what Kant calls "a broad-minded way of thinking" (*erweiterter Denkungsart*) when man "sets himself apart from the subjective private conditions of the judgment, within which so many others are as if bracketed, and reflects on his own judgment from *a universal standpoint* (which he can only determine by putting himself into the standpoint of others)" (175).

In German (as in the English translation), this standpoint is literally the place where one stands to see (*Standpunkt*).[24] Yet for it to be said to be universal (*allgemein*), it is not enough for him to situate himself in one or another's place (who is himself most often closed up in his subjectivity); it is not enough for him to come to occupy the very place of the other's equally captive point of view. Rather, as Kant stated before his digression devoted to the three maxims, what is necessary is that this point of view adopt that of all the others. Or more precisely, that of *every other*: This is the idea of a faculty of judgment

> that in its reflection takes account [*Rücksicht nimmt*] (*a priori*) of everyone else's way of representing in thought [*auf die Vorstellungsart jedes andern*] in order *as it were* [*gleichsam*] to hold its judgment up to human reason as a whole and thereby avoid the illusion which, from subjective private conditions that could easily be held to be objective, would have a detrimental influence on the judgment. Now this happens by one holding his judgment up not so much to the actual as to the merely possible [*bloss mögliche*] judgments of others, and putting himself into the position of every other [*in die Stelle jedes andern*]. (*Critique of the Power of Judgment*, 173–74, translation modified)

It is difficult to render all of the nuances and resonance of Kant's German, however important they are for us. When he speaks of "taking account" of the vision of the other, of every other, Kant says: *Rücksicht nehmen auf*. As if, literally, one had to double one's own gaze with a *glance back toward the other*, toward every other, so that this gaze might also be *regard for* him. If translation can obviously not render the complex circulation of regards and gazes proper to the German, one nonetheless has to wonder why, when Kant speaks of "the position of every other," the French translators think that they have to specify that this is about "every other human being."[25]

This drive or compulsion to limit the open and undetermined entirety of "every other" (*jedes andern*) is actually the whole question. On the one hand, nothing indicates that every other, with the others, makes for a whole, gathers together with them in a collective that could be deemed "humanity" in its entirety. And, on the other hand, when Kant speaks of holding the judgment "as it were" (*gleichsam*) up to "human reason as a whole" (*die gesamte Menschenvernunft*), one might wonder—a bit as Kant himself will, in the *Anthropology*, about the human species and its characteristics—if it is possible to think something like this, human-reason-as-a-whole, without however virtual or philosofictive a comparison with nonhuman reason.

Kant, of course, does not state things this way, or at least not in these particular pages. But these pages from the *Critique of the Power of Judgment* are not, any more than are others, isolable from the entire Kantian discourse. This discourse, as we have seen, has to evoke the wholly other that is neither human nor earthly, but also neither divine nor animal, in order to think, in its differential or comparative identity, the reason of the reasonable beings that we are.

That said, the restricting precision the French translators believed they needed to add concords and concurs with what we will now have to measure: It may well be that Kant himself was subject to a kind of repression or denial of the possibility of extraterrestrial reason. Not in the sense that its existence—which remains beyond the bounds of experience *up until today*, but not *a priori and forever*—would be attested and then denied. But in the sense that his philosofictive evocation, however necessary it may be and according to a necessity that leaves traces in so many of Kant's texts, is nonetheless regularly masked to the advantage of judgment's humanization or repatriation on earth.

This does not keep the question from insisting and persisting: in order to think, in order to take *every other* [*tout autre*] into account, is it not necessary, whether explicitly or implicitly, whether in an avowed or hidden manner, to have recourse to the philosofiction *of the wholly other* [*du tout-autre*]?

Return to Earth (with Extraterrestrials in the Footnotes)

In his *Theory of the Heavens*, Kant, as you will remember, concluded his long review of extraterrestrial modes of existence with the following words: "When one has filled one's mind with such observations"—meaning once one has thoroughly gazed out at and scanned, as Kant has just done over the course of the previous pages, the vast hierarchical system that "inhabitants of these distant celestial bodies" may form—"the view of the starry sky on a clear night gives one a kind of pleasure that only noble souls feel" (307).

In this 1755 piece of writing, it is as if the exobiological[26] speculations had in a way to *prepare* the mind for the satisfaction it will feel when faced with the spectacle of a sky filled with stars. For in the German syntax of this phrase (*wenn . . . so*), there certainly does seem to be a link from cause to effect, or at least a relation of consecution, between these speculations and this satisfaction.

In *The Critique of the Power of Judgment*, thirty-five years later, the same celestial spectacle is an occasion for speculations of an entirely different order. After the critical turn, aesthetics, with its pure judgments of taste, must be insularized or isolated in its purity; it must be detached from any dependent tie to any speculative and reasoned conceptuality. This is so much the case that the hypothesis of extraterrestrial life must be disqualified and excluded from aesthetic experience:

> If someone calls the sight of the starry heavens *sublime*, he must not ground such a judging of it on concepts of worlds inhabited by rational beings, taking the bright points with which we see the space above us to be filled as their suns, about which they move in their purposively appointed orbits, but must take it, as we see it . . . and it must be merely under this representation that we posit the sublimity that a pure aesthetic judgment attributes to this object. ("General Remark on the Exposition of Aesthetic Reflective Judgments," 148)

The extraterrestrials have disappeared, they've been pushed out of the earthly sublime and had to go back home so that they would not disturb the rigorous demands of the critical isolation of the faculties, to avoid the risk that reason and taste might encroach on each other. It is as if Kant, since the writings of his youth (which he did not always sign with his name, as was the case for *Theory of the Heavens,* which appeared without any mention of an author), had had to reterritorialize aesthetic experience on Earth and among humans.

When one compares writing as distant and as different as *Theory of the Heavens* and the *Critique of the Power of Judgment,* one might think that, if inhabitants of other worlds no longer have a place in the *Critique,* this is because they were a mere youthful fantasy or naïveté that Kant renounced in his critical maturity, that he had forgotten it or even disavowed or repressed it.

Yet the persistence of the extraterrestrial motif all the way into Kant's last work (*Anthropology*), its regular return in diverse forms (certainly less literal than in the *Theory of the Heavens*) prevents us from thinking that this was a mere reverie Kant indulged only once. In addition, as we saw over the course of our reading of the Third Critique, the question of the universal point of view cannot be easily contained or confined on Earth. Or at least one can legitimately wonder about the border, the limit that would stop the expansion of perspective, that would put an end to the expansion of judgments toward an "expanded way of thinking": Would it (not) be necessary to include, beyond the other as an alter ego, the *wholly other*?

Even if one thought one could limit the critique of judgment to Earth and its Earthlings, it would tend structurally to escape it, like that humanity that, in the *Anthropology*, will only be able to be characterized through recourse to an extra-earthly comparison. And it so happens that it is this same necessity of comparative departure from earth that we are now going to find again in other of Kant's texts where it is a question of a *cosmopolitan point of view*.

)) ((

In an essay dating from 1784, just before the Third Critique in "Idea for a Universal History with a Cosmopolitan Purpose,"²⁷ Kant's question indeed bears on the perspective to adopt so as to take in the view of the functioning of human actions insofar as they are the product of free will: "If it examines the free exercise of the human will *on a large scale*," is history, the historical narrative that tells of its manifestations, up to the task of "discover [ing] a regular progression"? (41). Is it possible to situate oneself in a perspective such that, by going beyond "what strikes us in the actions of individuals as confused and fortuitous," something like a "steadily advancing but slow development of man's original capacities" can appear "in the history of the entire species"? (41).

It is thus yet again a question of the human species, that is to say of a global or broad point of view capable of considering it as such, in its historical opening. And it is the philosopher's task to interrogate the *possibility* of such a point of view, of a view like a bird's eye's, that others would then be able to adopt:

We can scarcely help feeling a certain distaste on observing the activities [of humans] as enacted in the great world-drama, for we find that, despite the apparent wisdom of individual actions here and there, everything as a whole is made up of folly and childish vanity, and often of childish malice and destructiveness. The result is that we do not know what sort of opinion we should form of our species, which is so proud of its supposed superiority. The only way out for the philosopher, since he cannot assume that mankind follows any rational *purpose of its own* in its collective actions, is for him to attempt to discover a *purpose in nature* behind this senseless course of human events, and decide whether it is after all possible to formulate in terms of a definite plan of nature a history of creatures who act without a plan of their own. Let us now see if we can succeed in finding a guiding principle for such a history, and then leave it to nature to produce someone capable of writing it along the lines suggested. Thus nature produced a Kepler who found an unexpected means of reducing the eccentric orbits of the planets to definite laws, and a Newton who explained these laws in terms of a universal natural cause. ("Universal History," 42)

The position of the philosopher is not exactly situated *at the very point* of this encompassing or panoramic point of view. It consists rather in interrogating its principle. In other words, to extend the astronomical metaphor Kant is preparing in this passage and that he will develop later on, the philosopher is not in the position of a Kepler or a Newton of human history: Instead, he questions the possibility of their being born and seeing.

In Kant's eyes, this view or this point of view is possible: Yes, he says, we can think, and no doubt *we must* think that humanity develops over the course of its history toward a "perfect civil union" ("Universal History," Ninth Proposition, 51); that this is the "plan of nature" for it, in other words, the foundation of a cosmopolitan legislation "in which every state, even the smallest, could expect to derive its security and rights not from its own power or its own legal judgment, but solely from this great federation" ("Universal History," Seventh Proposition, 47). In to-day's terms, one would perhaps say that what Kant is attempting to imagine here is a just form of globalization founded on univer-sally just institutions.

But this becoming-world of the world, its union in a world that is one and just (that is, *justly one*) cannot be thought by Kant, almost in spite of himself, without recourse to fiction in general and to the philosofiction of *other worlds* in particular. Right after having affirmed at the beginning of the "Ninth Propo-sition" that it was possible to consider human history as targeting the political union of and within the species, Kant continues:

> It is admittedly a strange and at first sight absurd proposition to write a *history* according to an idea of how world events must develop if they are to conform to certain rational ends; it would seem that only a *novel* could result from such premises. Yet if it may be assumed that nature does not work without a plan and purposeful end, even amidst the arbitrary play of human freedom, this idea might nevertheless prove useful. And although we are too shortsighted to perceive the hidden mechanism of nature's scheme, this idea may yet serve as a guide to us in representing an otherwise planless *aggregate* of human actions as conforming, at least when considered as a whole, to a *system*. ("Universal History," 52)

The cosmopolitan point of view that affords systematic order for the history of humanity's progress toward a League of Nations, this point of view expanded by comparison with indi-vidual actions and nonetheless too shortsighted to pierce the secret of collective regulation, this aim or vision [*visée ou vision*], in short, this *Idea* is a fiction. A useful and utilizable novel. It's an *as if*, a *why not* that, in a performative way, will *effictively* pro-duce the possibility of that necessary point of view.[28] Kant expli-citly states as much at the beginning of his "Eighth Proposition": The fictional idea of the "hidden plan" destined to come to fruition in a complete and planetary cosmopolitanism, this vision, worthy of a "political prophecy" ("Universal History," 52, translation modified) or of a philosophical "millenarianism" itself contributes to its own realization merely by being stated. In this case, there is something we might describe as an *effictive* buckle of ideal fiction:

> *The history of the human race as a whole can be regarded as the realization of a hidden plan of nature to bring about a . . . perfect political constitution as the only possible state within which all natural capacities of mankind can be developed completely.* This proposition follows from the previous one. [In effect, in the "seventh proposition," Kant has just offered the hypothesis that even wars and other of humanity's woes force it nonetheless to progress toward cosmopolitanism.] We can see that philosophy too may have its *chiliastic* expectations; but they are of such a kind that fulfillment can be hastened, if only indirectly, by a knowledge of the idea they are based on. ("Universal History," 50)

This chiliastic, prophetic, or simply fictive point of view thus repeatedly labors, in a certainly discrete way, toward the effectiveness of its own fiction.

But the effectiveness of this *as if*, its *effiction*, also passes through the philosofiction of other worlds and of extraterrestrial life. When he continues by wondering "whether experience can discover anything to indicate a purposeful natural process of this kind" ("Universal History," 50), Kant answers once again through a cosmological analogy: that of the cyclical rotation of the planets. It is thus as if, according to a necessity of Kantian discourse that can be constantly verified, the cosmopolitan called for the cosmological:

> For this cycle of events [of possible progress] seems to take so long a time to complete, that the small part of it traversed by

mankind up till now does not allow us to determine with certainty the shape of the whole cycle, and the relation of the parts to the whole. It is no easier than it is to determine, from all hitherto available astronomical observations, the path which our sun with its whole swarm of satellites is following within the vast system of the fixed stars; although from the general premise that the universe is constituted as a system and from the little which has been learnt by observation, we can conclude with sufficient certainty that a movement of this kind does exist in reality. ("Universal History," 50)

We will soon see that this cyclical nature of human affairs, as a figure for the regularity that is only visible from very far away, will also accompany the pages Kant dedicates to the French Revolution in the second part of the *Conflict of the Faculties* (1797). But in the pages we are currently reading, in this 1784 essay on the "Idea of Universal History," it is ultimately the problem of universal law and justice on Earth, which, in order to be thought as such, must be situated, in however fictive a way, in relation to and within the horizon of the hypothesis of extraterrestrial life. In effect, in a note, Kant once again explicitly appeals to exobiological philosofiction; let's read the surprising footnote at the bottom of the page, taking our time for it to come from within the main text:

If he lives among others of his own species, man is *an animal who needs a master*. For he certainly abuses his freedom in relation to others of his own kind. And even although, as a rational creature, he desires a law to impose limits on the freedom of all, he is still misled by his self-seeking animal inclinations into exempting himself from the law where he can. He thus requires a *master* to break his self-will and force him to obey a universally valid will under which everyone can be free. But where is he to find such a master? Nowhere else but in the human species. But this master will also be an animal who needs a master. Thus while man may try as he will, it is hard to see how he can obtain for public justice a supreme authority which would itself be just, whether he seeks this authority in a single person or in a group of many persons selected for this purpose. For each one of them will always misuse his freedom if he does not have anyone above him to apply force to him as the laws should require it. Yet the highest authority has to be just *in itself* and yet also a *man*. This is therefore the most difficult of all tasks, and a perfect solution is impossible. Nothing straight can be constructed from warped wood as that which man is made of. Nature only requires of us that we should approximate to this idea.*

*Man's role is thus a highly artificial one. We do not know how it is with the inhabitants of other planets and with their nature, but if we ourselves execute this commission of nature well, we may surely flatter ourselves that we occupy no mean status among our neighbors in the cosmos. Perhaps their position is such that each individual can fulfill his destiny completely within his own lifetime. With us it is otherwise; only the species as a whole can hope for this. (46–47)

What a strange passage this is, where extraterrestrials are seen turning up out of the blue. From the main text to this note on the inhabitants of other planets, there is apparently a leap.

Where do they come from, these living beings from other worlds, and why do they choose to turn up here and now, in these particular lines? At first, one gets the impression that Kant's discourse all of sudden and arbitrarily bounds across an abyssal distance, as if it were crossing in one intergalactic leap or spurt from one universe to another. Yet the light-years that separate the satellite note from its textual center of gravity—this distance that seems infinite dwindles if one lends an ear to what already in the main text, even if discreetly and in a kind of smuggling, calls out to reasonable beings from other worlds: the chief, the master, the earthly sovereign, says Kant, must be a man; the one who should be able to overlook the humanity of men to lead them toward their goal, which they do not know, this one must himself be taken from and included in the human species. This is the impossible to which Earthlings are condemned, so much so that they will reach their destination or their definition (in German, *Bestimmung* means both) only *at the limit* of their infinitely deferred becoming. Unlike extraterrestrials that, for their part, incarnate the possibility of a self-coincidence that does not await the fleeting horizon of generations, throughout eternity.

Somewhat as in Kant's *Anthropology*, where there will emerge an impossible demand for a comparative element that would allow the human species to be characterized, here, the nonearthly reasonable being, the *alien* appears as the border and the tangent toward which humanity tends, asymptotically, as a way of finding itself. It is in or on the basis of the extraterrestrial that humanity could be embodied, define itself as such, and arrive at the end of the journey that carries it away on the spaceship the planet Earth is, according to Carl Schmitt's expression that I commented on at length.

It is now clear: The reference to extraterrestrials is no longer as meteoric in its emergence as it might have seemed on first reading. It is not isolated and arbitrary, but quite to the contrary corresponds to a profound logic that runs throughout all of Kant's work, even if in an underground (we might say an *underearthly*) way. In the opening of the gap between a main text and a footnote satellite that gravitates around it, what is announced is, in effect, *the necessity of thinking humanity based on its extra-earthly limit.*

Of course, compared to the *Theory of the Heavens*, this necessity now has trouble finding its place in Kantian discourse: The extraterrestrials are driven away, contained and confined to the reduced space of a strange footnote satellite. But their return is only all the more symptomatic. And their necessity only seems all the more intractable.

)) ((

In what way, then, *with an eye to what*, are they necessary, these Kantian *aliens*?

With an eye to a certain view: with a view onto that cosmopolitan gaze whose unearthly condition of possibility must have been glimpsed by Kant already in his *Theory of the Heavens* and which he repeatedly interrogated in a low voice, all the way through his *Anthropology*, in the margins of his major writing. And as it happens, as we've unearthed the pages where this gaze is being sought, marked, and inscribed, we have not only begun to take big steps through the entirety of Kant's oeuvre, from one of the first to one of the last works. Following a path that was struck in part by Hannah Arendt, we have also and above all sketched out a pathway from the aesthetic to the political by way of a speculative cosmology: By going backwards in the classical chronology of the time of reading, it is as if the articulation, the link, the hinge between the subjective universality of the *Critique of the Power of Judgment* and the cosmopolitanism of the "Idea of Universal History" resided in the cosmic vision of the *Theory of Heaven*. As if the *each-and-every-one* on the basis of which the judgment of taste is oriented could include humanity as such only when taking a cosmotheoretical detour through the *wholly other* that inhabits extraterrestrial globes.

After this detour that we still must complete, we will need to recall our geostrategic considerations under the guidance of a reading of Carl Schmitt. And what will then be announced or opened up to us will be, at the intersection of the aesthetic and the political—or better yet: of *cosmetics* and *cosmopolitics*—the terrain where a war is being waged whose stakes are a veritable *geopolitics of the sensible*.

CHAPTER 3 *Cosmetics and Cosmopolitics*

Where are we with it all?

Where do we come from and where are we going?

We have covered quite a bit of ground, starting with the discovery of the new earthly world as described by Carl Schmitt, which has led us to Kantian cosmopolitics as seen from the extraterrestrial perspective of the inhabitants of those other new worlds in the still unexplored stars of the cosmos that surrounds [*entoure*] us. Or rather that *etches us out* [*détoure*], as one can say in the vocabulary of the digital treatment of images as a way of naming the action of delimiting or circumscribing a detail— the detail that we are, according to Nietzsche, "in some remote corner of the universe, which has been poured out glimmering in countless solar systems."[1]

I would like to take advantage of the feeling of weightlessness that is starting to come over us and *suspend* our trajectory for a moment. To let it float a bit for an interlude, to let it drift toward the territories of science fiction. We should be able to come back with a sharpened gaze more attentive *to our sight*, to what constitutes our point of view.

The Other's Very Gaze

Jack Finney's story *The Invasion of the Body Snatchers*[2] has been adapted to film several times, in particular by Don Siegel and

Abel Ferrera. The invaders here are "space spores," as the novel says, spores contained in vegetal envelopes that fall from the sky and, as one character puts it, "looked to me like very large seed pods" (145). These spores have the capacity to duplicate perfectly, "cell by . . . cell," any form of life they encounter in the culture where they fall. For example, humans, Earthlings. This is what is explained by the botanist and biologist Bernard Budlong, who, like so many others, was a victim of this *identical transformation*, if one can put it this way. And his explanation is also a judgment on the limits of our imagination, which condemns us everywhere to seeing only ourselves:

> "So in a sense, of course, the pods are a parasite on whatever life they encountered," Budlong went on [whose name also of course recalls the "bud"]. "But they are the perfect parasite, capable of far more than clinging to the host. They . . . have the ability to re-form and reconstitute themselves into perfect duplication, cell for living cell, of any life form they may encounter in whatever conditions that life has suited itself for." . . . Budlong . . . held up a hand. "I know; it sounds like gibbering— insane raving. That's only natural. Because we're trapped by our own conceptions, . . . our necessarily limited notions of what life can be. Actually, we can't really conceive of anything very much different from ourselves. . . . Prove it yourself; what do imaginary men from Mars, in our comic strips and fiction, resemble? Think about it. They resemble grotesque versions of *ourselves*—we can't imagine anything different! Oh, they may have six legs, three arms, and antennae sprouting from their heads," he smiled, "like insects, we're familiar with. But they are nothing fundamentally different from what we know." He held up a finger, as though reproving an unprepared pupil. (174)

This kind of discourse may seem surprising coming from the mouth of a character in a science fiction novel who distinguishes himself from others not by insisting on the extraterrestrials' differences, but by highlighting, on the contrary, their ability to become absolutely indistinct from us. We understand, however, that the stakes of this *metamorphosis without change* undergone by the humans duplicated by the spores are the limits of humanity. In other words, humanity's characteristics and contours are exposed from their identical reproduction. As if we could observe and define ourselves as we are only on the basis of this exercise in mirroring cloning, even as it also dooms us to seek out what is different in our clone. Which, apparently, is *nothing*.

The hero and narrator, a doctor by the name of Miles Bennell, ends up understanding, he thinks, what distinguishes humans from the duplicates that replace them: emotion. Yes, the expression of passion or affects, this is what was lacking in those reproduced humans. This is so much the case that in order to attempt to escape from the vegetal metamorphosis threatening them, Miles and his companion Becky Driscoll, will have to *hide* their feelings. While fleeing a city besieged from the inside by this strange mutation that leaves each one unchanged, they will have to feign indifference to indifferentiate themselves from the threatening clones that they encounter:

> Half a dozen yards ahead, a man slid out of the front seat of a parked car and stood waiting for us, a man in uniform, a policeman, Sam Pink. I didn't let us break stride or hesitate, and we walked up to him and stopped. "Well, Sam," I said *dully*, "now we're with you, and it's not so bad." . . . He stood staring at me, turning over in his mind what I'd said. I waited, *uninterested*. (201, emphasis mine)

Once one goes from the novel to the screen, this is thus the handsome challenge of this plot, of this critique of science fiction through science fiction: How can one show this in images? How can one *bring indifference or indifferentiation* to be remarked?

There are of course many American films produced in the context of the Cold War that present this glazed-over look, the absence of emotions in individuals manipulated by an extraterrestrial power, which one quickly understands as a transparent allegory of Soviet totalitarianism. One could think of *Invaders from Mars* (William Cameron Menzies, 1953) or of *Earth vs. The Flying Saucers* (Fred F. Sears, 1956). In comparison to these B movies, what gives *Invasion of the Body Snatchers*, directed in 1956 by Don Siegel, its strength and originality is the trouble the protagonists Miles (Kevin McCarthy) and Becky (Dana Wynter) have acting, that is, *allowing indifference to be seen.* Thus—in a detail that the screenplay writer or director *had* to add in relation to Finley's novel—when the young woman sees a dog about to be run over by a passing truck, she can't keep herself from screaming. At this point, the camera shows the *gaze* of the identically cloned cop three different times and with insistence as he stares at the runaway couple. As if the director's lens were desperately trying to grasp the ungraspable difference between difference and indifference, the indistinct distinction that cannot be seen but that instead *looks out at us, concerns us [nous regarde].*

Right from the beginning of the plot, in the novel, it is a question of gazes. When Miles and Becky go to visit Wilma, who, without knowing anything yet, suspects her Uncle Ira of no

Invasion of the Body Snatchers (Don Siegel, 1956)

Invasion of the Body Snatchers (Don Siegel, 1956)

longer being her uncle, the invisible and indifferent difference is housed in the eyes; as Wilma declares: "Uncle Ira was a father to me, from infancy, and when he talked about my childhood, Miles, there was—always—a special look in his eyes. . . . Miles, that look, way in back of the eyes, is gone" (21). How then can one show this difference in the way of looking? How can one show a point of view, the point of view of that other or of that wholly other that merges with us and on the basis of which *we* are characterized in *our* difference?

In *Body Snatchers* (1993), Abel Ferrara ends up turning away from the register of sight, and in an incredible way, yet not without having insisted on gazes, and to such an extent that rarely will a film have pushed me, as a spectator, to try to look its actors right in the eye. Yet at the same time, it was a wasted effort; in effect, under my very eyes and in theirs, there was *visibly* no difference at all.

In Ferrara's film, it is no longer Becky and Miles but Marti (Gabrielle Anwar) and Tim (Billy Worth) who attempt to flee a military camp invaded by the spores turned humanoid. Marti is detained in the military hospital and is in the process of being transformed, her duplication almost complete when Tim comes and liberates her *in extremis*. They are about to return to Tim's helicopter and also feign indifference in order not to be noticed, when an officer gives orders with his inexpressive look. This time, the runaway couple crosses paths with Jenn, Marti's friend, who tells her that her little brother Andy is looking for her. Marti and Jenn look at each other for a long time, *visibly indifferent*, before going their separate ways. But Marti turns around, unable to suppress a question: Where is he? Where's Andy?

It's at this point that, giving up on the task of *showing* the difference—the ungraspable difference between difference and indifference—Abel Ferrara chooses to allow it to resonate as a terrifying scream. An *insane* scream that neither says nor states anything, that only tears into the soundtrack and seems to

Body Snatchers (Abel Ferrara, 1993)

Body Snatchers (Abel Ferrara, 1993)

Body Snatchers (Abel Ferrara, 1993)

Body Snatchers (Abel Ferrara, 1993)

Body Snatchers (Abel Ferrara, 1993)

lacerate the image as the helicopter propellers turn like razors at the end of Jenn's pointing finger while she screams. It is an intolerable scream that designates and *signs* what we would not be able to see without our gaze itself being ripped apart: ourselves, us humans, in our difference retraced from the perspective of the wholly other, so similar to us.

Unless it is not also this torn gaze, traversed by our difference as humans, impossible to situate, that quite precisely allows us to see. To have a point of view.

)) ((

It is impossible to see what rips our gaze apart. Yet it is no doubt impossible to see without this rip that inhabits our gaze and constitutes it.

A vein of science fiction movies struggles in an exemplary way with the aporia we have started to read in Kant: If the aesthetic point of view implies its universalization, and if this universalizing goal implies in turn a cosmopolitics determined by the philosofiction of the wholly other, then these implications are also folded back *into the gaze*, to complicate it by marking within it the fold of an internal difference that only becomes visible *at the limit*.

This kind of limit is explored by John Carpenter's 1988 film *They Live*: the cross-eyed limit, if one can put it this way, inherent in the gaze. And which immediately turns it into a cosmopolitical issue.

The protagonist, a certain John Nada (Roddy Piper), arrives in Los Angeles, a city devastated by unemployment and poverty. He finds a temporary job on a construction site and spends his nights on an empty lot where the homeless struggle to survive as best they can. He soon notices that, in the little neighboring church, something strange is going on. Under the cover of holding choir rehearsals, which is actually just a recorded tape, a group of men is preparing an uprising against "them," the ones in power. By sending the Earthlings subliminal messages—hidden in advertising posters, books, newspapers or TV shows—"they" are constantly

They Live (John Carpenter, 1988)

They Live (John Carpenter, 1988)

recalling us to order; their injunctions, which we read and see everywhere without knowing it, are "obey," "consume," "don't think."

In a box he finds in the little church, John finds a pair of sunglasses. And when he puts them on, not only do the subliminal messages appear to him in black and white, but the world, which itself becomes black and white, is divided into those whose faces do not change—humans, Earthlings—and extraterrestrials with bony faces that look like X-rayed skeletons. To John's newly equipped eyes, an elegant elderly lady shopping in her fur coat, for example, turns out to be one of the creatures governing our world by enforcing its law of submissive consummation. When

They Live (John Carpenter, 1988)

John starts to insult her, the other invaders in the store get it: He sees; he truly sees. He's dangerous.

So John gets found out and becomes a wanted man: The extraterrestrials signal his presence with their watch-radios or try to find him using little flying objects, drones equipped with an artificial eye.[3] "What do these things want?" asks one of John's acolytes, who, like John, has joined the clandestine, earthly resistance. Another one answers, "They're free-enterprisers. The Earth is just another developing planet. Their third world."

Science fiction here is the extraterrestrial projection of human, earthly politics: The invaders are ourselves and our capitalist consumer society; in a classic plot device, the aliens incarnate our alienation. Yet beyond this traditionally futuristic gesture, if one can put it this way, *They Live* radicalizes in particular the staging of this extraterrestrial point of view, one that literally partitions Earthlings' gazes: sometimes it inhabits their gaze and overlaps with it; at other times it divides it. So much so that the gaze as it is constructed in the film is in a way constitutively cross-eyed. Within one sequence, earthly views are constantly doubled or redoubled [*redoublés ou dédoublées*] by the vision that opens from the point of view of the other.

It is thus as if a gaze, in order to be a gaze, necessarily had to be at least double, marked in some way by the perspective of others. As if it had to allow itself to be cut into [*entamé*] by the other's gaze, by an *exchange of views* that must inhabit any view in order to make it possible, in order to constitute it as a point of view. In short, as if a point of view could only institute itself and stand if it includes within itself a certain *reflection* of the wholly other.

This is also, as we shall see, the crux of the philosofictive plot we are getting ready to read once again in Kant. A tale—almost a series or a feuilleton—whose episodes we will have to reconstruct, given the fact that they are divided into several volumes, from *The Theory of the Heavens* to the *Conflict of the Faculties* by way of a return to *The Critique of the Power of Judgment* and the "philosophical sketch" called *Perpetual Peace*.

From the Plurality of Worlds to the Revolution

The tradition Kant joins with his *Theory of the Heavens* and then with the unexpected yet recurrent arrival of extraterrestrials in his later texts is complex and sinuous and has many branches. Notwithstanding the breaks that change its course, it persists, starting at least with Epicurus and continuing through Kepler (who spoke of the inhabitants of the Moon as "Endymionides") by way of Plutarch, Nicholas of Cusa, and many others. Before reaching, with Fontenelle, what is no doubt its peak.[4]

Devoted to the subject of "inhabitants of the stars," the appendix to Kant's *Theory of the Heavens*[5] quite explicitly recalls this tradition. Kant immediately cites Christian Huygens, the author of *Kosmotheoros* ("spectator of the universe"), published in The Hague in 1698; Huygens himself cites Fontanelle. Kant writes:

> The satirical view of the wit in The Hague[6] who, after reporting the general news from the realm of the sciences, was able to present in a ridiculous way the notion of the necessary population of all the celestial bodies, can only be approved of. "Those creatures," he says, "that inhabit the forests on the head of a beggar had long regarded their abode as an

immeasurable sphere and themselves as the masterpiece of creation when one of them, whom heaven had endowed with a finer soul, a little *Fontenelle* of his species, suddenly became aware of the head of a nobleman. He immediately called all the wits of his quarter together and said to them with delight: we are not the only living beings in all of nature; behold here a new country, *more lice live here.*" . . . Let us judge without prejudice. This insect that expresses the disposition of most people very well both in the way it lives and in its insignificance, can be used as a comparison with good reason. Because in its imagination its existence matters infinitely to nature; it considers the whole of the rest of creation as in vain as far as it does not have its species as a precise goal, as the centre point of its purposes. (Kant, *Theory of the Heavens,* 296–97)

"Let us judge without prejudice," Kant thus concludes immediately after having named or cited two eminent representatives of the tradition we could call pluriworldist. This indicates just how much, already in *Theory of the Heavens,* judgment is one of the great themes that pluriworldism seems destined to nourish in Kant's work, so much so that the passages we read from his later writings, from the "Idea of a Universal History" through the *Anthropology*, could all be placed under the sign of the narrator's response to the marquise in Fontanelle's *Interviews*:

We want to judge everything, and we're always at a bad vantage point. We want to judge ourselves, we're too close; we want to judge others, we're too far away. If one could be between the Earth and the Moon, that would be the proper place to see them well. One should simply be a spectator of the world, not an inhabitant.[7]

In one or another turn of phrase, it is incredible to see just how much Fontenelle seems to anticipate the great Kantian themes related to the plurality of inhabited worlds: not only judgment, but also the interaction between imagination and reason, those two faculties that, as we will see, are said to play freely in the experience of the sublime as Kant will describe it in the *Critique of the Power of Judgment*. One gets the impression of being faced with a draft or a sketch of Kantian discourse on the sublime while reading this bit of dialogue between the narrator and the marquise:

> "My reason is pretty well convinced," said the Marquise, "but my imagination's overwhelmed by the infinite multitude of inhabitants on all these planets, and perplexed by the diversity one must establish among them; for I can see that Nature . . . will have made them all different. But how can one picture all that?"
>
> "It's not up to the imagination to attempt to picture all that," I answered. "It is not proper for the imagination to go any farther than the eyes can. One may only perceive by a kind of universal vision the diversity which Nature must have placed among all the worlds."[8]

We will therefore be returning to the play between reason and imagination in the Kantian constitution of this very "universal vision." As for judgment and the maxim that states, *Let us judge without prejudice*—as a spectator of the universe, as a *kosmotheoros* would rather than as an inhabitant of the world—this is, as we have seen, the great affair of the critique of taste. Yet Kant will also lay claim to this *cosmotheoretical* perspective for judgment (that must be disinterested and susceptible to adopting the point of view of every other, if not of the wholly other) in the *Conflict of the Faculties* on the basis of the example of the French Revolution. There it will be a question of thinking about the posture of a spectator who is not engaged in the course of the world and who in this sense does not inhabit it. Only this detached observer, this *noninhabitant of the world* will be able to see it through the just point of view.

)) ((

The second section of the *Conflict of the Faculties* opens with the following question: "Is the human race continually progressing?" This is an echo of the question in "The Idea of a Universal History." But, Kant wonders as he immediately reformulates the question, "What do we *want* to know in this matter?" Perhaps quite simply a prophecy, a guess about what is awaiting humanity: "We desire a fragment of human history and one, indeed, that is drawn not from past but future time, therefore a *predictive* history."[9]

Yet because experience cannot provide a fragment of history yet to come, and because there is not any point of view of reason that could look out over freely accomplished future actions (this, says Kant in a passage we've already read, "would be the standpoint of providence which is situated beyond all human wisdom," a kind of point of view seen from "the sun" [*Conflict of the Faculties*, 300] that could discern the regularity of the course of the apparently insane planets that we are), because there is thus nothing that would allow us to read in advance this unwritten historical narrative, the only remaining element of the answer is the following: "There must be some experience in the human race which, as an event, points to the disposition and capacity of the human race to be the cause of its own advance toward the better, and (since this should be the act of a being endowed with freedom), toward the human race as being author of this advance" (301). What will this event be that could be seen as an "intimation," a "*historical sign*" allowing us to conclude that progress is a "*tendency* within the human race viewed in its entirety"? (301, emphasis mine).

The event in question is the French Revolution.[10] Or rather, it is not the revolution in and of itself but its *spectacle*. Or even better and even more precisely, the event is *the point of view* of its spectators, sympathizing with it from afar and publicly expressing their sympathy.

In short, this event is, we could say, an *aesthetic* event. Not, of course, in the sense that the revolution would be beautiful or ugly (it is certainly not a question for Kant, to take up Benjamin's famous phrase, of aestheticizing politics), but in the sense that the cosmopolitical importance of revolution and its significance in terms of the progress of the human race essentially depend on an uninterested and universally communicable perspective—in other words, on a judgment for which the critique of taste constitutes a kind of propaedeutic:

> This occurrence consists neither in momentous deeds nor crimes committed by human beings whereby what was great among human beings is made small or what was small is made great, nor in ancient splendid political structures which vanish as if by magic while others come forth in their place as if from the depths of the earth. No, nothing of the sort. It is simply the mode of thinking of the spectators which reveals itself *publicly* in this game of great revolutions, and manifests such a universal yet disinterested sympathy for the players on one side against those on the other, even at the risk that this partiality would become very disadvantageous from them if discovered. Owing to its universality, this mode of thinking demonstrates a character of the human race at large and all at once; owing to its disinterestedness, a moral character of humanity. . . . The revolution of a gifted people which we have seen unfolding in our day may succeed or miscarry; it may be filled with misery and atrocities to the point that a right-thinking human being, were he boldly to hope to execute it successfully the second time, would never resolve to make the experiment at such cost—this revolution, I say, nonetheless finds in the hearts of all spectators (who are not engaged in this game themselves) a wishful *participation* that borders closely on enthusiasm the very expression of which is fraught with danger; this sympathy, therefore, can

have no other cause than a moral predisposition in the human race. (Kant, *Conflict*, 301–2)

The event is thus not the event itself, but its *public* nature: Its site is not the scene of action, but the publicity of this "uninvolved public looking on" who "sympathized . . . without the least intention of assisting" (303). This is where something took place, a phenomenon that "*will not be forgotten*" (304), even if the goal of the revolution "should not now be attained," even if it "should finally fail," even if "everything should relapse into its former rut" (304).

It is thus the aesthetic dimension of the revolution—in the very precise sense we have indicated—that allows Kant to conclude:

> The human race has always been in progress toward the better and will continue to be henceforth. To him who does not consider what happens in just some one nation but also has regard to the whole scope of all the peoples on earth who will gradually come to participate in progress, this reveals the prospect of an immeasurable time. . . . (*Conflict*, 304)

Let us interrupt Kant's sentence here for an instant. Let us suspend it in order to underline that it is thus thanks to a gaze forged in the disinterested and universalizing aim of the judgment of taste, it is thanks to this aesthetic point of view that a revolution's movement of worldwide expansion can be envisaged or seen in advance. As is the case here and elsewhere, aesthetics gestures toward politics, while also and almost immediately recalling the philosofictive hypothesis that is now familiar to us; Kant thus goes on (I'm rewinding a bit to reread):

> This reveals the prospect of an immeasurable time—*provided* [my emphasis] at least that there does not . . . occur a second epoch of natural revolution which will push aside the human

race to clear the stage for other creatures [*andere Geschöpfe*], like that which . . . submerged the plant and animal kingdoms before human beings ever existed. (*Conflict*, 304–5)

As we can see and verify once again: If the cosmopolitical dimension of the revolution (the way it affects "the whole scope of all the peoples on earth") is in a way prepared and made possible by the aesthetic point of view forged in the critique of taste, it appears only by immediately involving the perspective of a wholly other yet to come. What Kant seems *bound* to envisage here, *in order to* be able to see the revolution with the eyes of a cosmotheoretical spectator not inhabiting the world, is the arrival of an unknown species that would take the place of Earthlings. For example in the wake of climate change (a *Naturrevolution*, as he says) that he is not far from describing—as if he were ventriloquizing in advance someone like today's Al Gore—in the terms of an *intrinsic* extraterrestrial threat.[11]

These aliens might thus come back one more time, in the guise of these "other creatures" who might supplant the human race thanks to a global upheaval comparable to the great climate changes of natural history that predate hominization. They might well land once again, thanks to an *unless* that, like all the *as if*'s and *why not*'s, continually and philosofictively marks the gaze of Kantian judgment when it is a question of "unbounded" perspectives.

As if—yes, *as if*—the opening of these perspectives that are inextricably cosmological, cosmotheoretical, and cosmopolitical needed the virtual presence of these extraterrestrials with their *effictive* gaze as a guarantee of this very opening.

)) ((

Such an opening perhaps converges with the very space of the Enlightenment. Which is precisely the space of public transparence, of luminous and entirely illuminated publicity, dissipating the shadows of superstition (it is "the public use of man's reason," says Kant, that is alone able to "bring about enlighten-ment among men").[12]

But Kantian extraterrestrials *are not* a superstition any more than they are divinized. To the contrary, they incarnate in an exemplary way a kind of necessary other side of human reason so that this reason may be thought in its light and as light, always and still yet to come. And this is why, in their recurring philoso-fiction, they also provide a figure for a certain enlightened idea of justice.

Without "the *formal attribute of publicness*," writes Kant in the second appendix of his "Philosophical Sketch" called *Perpetual Peace* (1795),[13] "there can be no justice." For justice can only be "conceived of as *publicly knowable*." This is why the transcenden-tal formula for public law is stated as follows:

> All actions . . . are wrong if their maxim is not compatible with their being made public. . . . For a maxim which I may not *declare openly* without thereby frustrating my own intention, or which must at all costs be *kept secret* if it is to succeed, or which I cannot *publicly acknowledge* without thereby inevita-bly arousing the resistance of everyone to my plans, can only have stirred up this necessary and general (hence *a priori* fore-seeable) opposition against me because it is itself unjust and thus constitutes a threat to everyone. (*Perpetual Peace*, 125–26)

Yet the only beings who, from this point of view, would be entirely fair or lawful would be those "reasonable beings" the *Anthropology* mentions: those creatures who, as you will remem-ber, might inhabit "some other planet," where they could only think "aloud" since they would be incapable of having "any thoughts that they did not at the same time *utter*."[14]

Beings, then, that are incapable of keeping a secret, of having nonilluminated, obscure plans. Beings that, in addition, could thus look at and observe each other, from planet to planet, as the marquise in Fontenelle's *Conversations* notes with pleasure: "I should amuse myself with pleasure with the idea of all the glasses of Jupiter being pointed towards the earth, as ours are toward him, and the mutual curiosity with which the planets consider one other and ask among themselves, *What world is that? What people live on it?*"[15]

)) ((

Like the marquise, one of the characters in the first silent Soviet science fiction film—*Aelita*, directed by Iakov Protazanov in 1924—dreams of seeing other worlds. It starts as a secret dream that is destined to become public thanks to a cosmopolitical revolution.

On Mars, in constructivist sets and costumes, Queen Aelita goes, *covertly*, toward the telescope that Gor, the "planet's guardian of energy," has made. With this apparatus, whose existence has to be kept secret, one can "observe life on other planets," as an intertitle explains. Subject to the same curiosity as the marquise, her earthly ancestor from the beginning of the Enlightenment, Queen Aelita begs Gor: "Show me the other worlds," she pleads, "no one will know." And she ends up getting what she desires.

One evening, the Martian queen thus secretly looks at Earth. And what we see through her gaze is archive footage showing our streets, the traffic in one of our cities, one of our ports where warships are stationed. Then, as a conclusion, there is a close-up of an Earthling like us, a certain Los, who is meeting his wife on a bridge in Moscow. Aelita is visibly fascinated by the kiss they exchange. And she asks Gor to put his lips to hers, "like the humans, out there, on the Earth."

A kiss seen from Mars is incredible. Seen through the utterly other eyes of the queen from out there, from her incomparable point of view, it seems incredible to us right here, down here. Never had a kiss appeared to us this way.

On Earth, Los is actually an engineer who directs the radio station in Moscow. He has just received a strange message that

Aelita (Yakov Protozanov, 1924)

Aelita (Yakov Protozanov, 1924)

remains incomprehensible to him. Los, who is secretly at work organizing a journey to Mars, imagines a possible message come from outer space. Often, says an intertitle, "his imagination suggested images to him."

The Earthling thus thinks of Mars; and the Martian thinks of the Earth. They each think of the other, secretly, without knowing it, according to a secret that is even secret from themselves. Yet at the same time, in this interplanetary shot and countershot that unveil them one by one, their secrets are no longer secret. They are inscribed in the space of cosmotheoretical publicity where the symmetry of their gazes and their aspirations is quickly redoubled by an implicit parallel between extraterrestrial politics and the politics of the Soviet Union in the 1920s. On Mars, there reigns a totalitarian regime where workers are exploited: They only occasionally ever leave the underground spaces where they work as slaves in order to be frozen as a way of preserving them for future tasks. On Earth, in contrast, in Moscow, long sequences insist on economic hardship and rationings, on the misappropriation of food and burgeoning profits on the black market.

When, one day, as all of Moscow is celebrating the revolution, Los ends up flying to Mars, as if he wanted to escape the commemorations of earthly memory, he is in reality traveling to encounter a repetition of the recent history of his planet. With Aelita's help, he will reedit what has already taken place on Earth: "Follow our example, comrades!" he cries to the proletarians of the solar system, "and found the Union of Socialist Republics of Mars!"

In the publicness of interplanetary space illuminated in this way, thanks to the event of a revolution that not only is not forgotten but extends even beyond all the "peoples of the Earth," we find a certain spirit of Kantian Enlightenment that seems to want to go beyond itself in its self-perpetuation. A triumph of reason, it would seem, in its emancipation on the other side of its earthly limits.

Their Sublime Suns (Humanity Raises the Anchor, Part 2)

And yet things are not quite so simple. Inhabitants of other planets are not merely relays or representatives of human and earthly reason that would allow us to project its enlightenment ever further into the night of the cosmos. Or rather, if they are, it is also as fictive beings, as products of a philosofictive imagination.

The true Kantian place or site for the extraterrestrial question may well be found somewhere in between imagination and reason. And if it is in between these two faculties that we must travel in order to hound out the Kantian aliens still hiding there, they may well be, in turn, able to return the light we cast on them in a new way onto the experience of the sublime that Kant defined precisely as the play between reason and imagination.

Of course, as you will remember, if, in *The Theory of the Heavens*, the extraterrestrial hypothesis participated in the noble pleasure taken while contemplating the starry sky, in the Third Critique, in contrast, the extraterrestrials were excluded from the experience of the sublime; they were rejected in a few dismissive phrases that sent them back home: "If someone calls the starry heavens *sublime*, he must not ground such a judging of it on concepts of worlds inhabited by rational beings, taking the bright points with which we see the space above us to be filled as their suns, about which they move in their purposively appointed orbits, but must take it, as we see it" (Kant, *Critique of the Power of Judgment*, 152).

And yet, if only in the guise of their expulsion or remarked absence, extraterrestrials will have nonetheless also passed through this text, as they do in many others. They will have left traces there, deeper traces than one might think.

In order to be up to the task of reading their footprints, we need to go back to the premises of Kant's discourse on the sublime.

)) ((

Almost thirty years before the Third Critique, Kant had considered the sublime in his 1764 *Observations on the Feeling of the Beautiful and the Sublime*. And his point of view in this text was rather peculiar since he declared right from the beginning, "I will cast my glance . . . more with the eye of an observer than of the philosopher."[16] This distinction would merit a lengthy discussion, for it is certainly not foreign to Kant's attitude toward extraterrestrials and toward the philosofictive role of the *noninhabitants of the world* he attributes to them in the constitution of a certain cosmotheoretical or cosmopolitan perspective. But let us turn rather without delay to the examples Kant gives to help distinguish the beautiful from the sublime; they provide an echo to the end of *The Theory of the Heavens* and announce more than one passage in the Third Critique:

> The night is *sublime*, the day is *beautiful*. Casts of mind that possess a feeling for the sublime are gradually drawn into lofty sentiments . . . of eternity, by the quiet calm of a summer evening, when the flickering light of the stars breaks through the umber shadows of the night and the lonely moon rises into view. . . . A long duration is sublime. If it is of time past, it is noble; if it is projected forth into an unforeseeable future, then there is something terrifying in it. . . . Haller's description of the future eternity inspires a mild horror, and of the past, a transfixed admiration. (*Observations*, 24–26; Albrecht von Haller [1708–1777], was a Swiss philosopher and scholar, author of an "Uncompleted poem on eternity," a kind of pluriworldist manifesto that Kant had already cited in his *Theory of the Heavens*)

The sublime, which Kant says "touches" while the beautiful "charms," is thus the feeling apparently destined to accompany philosofictions on the plurality of worlds as well as the cosmotheoretical contemplation of the planets, stars, galaxies, and their eternity, for, as Kant will reiterate many years later in his

Anthropology, the "*sublime* is awe-inspiring *greatness,*" a mixture of seduction and fear; if it is not "the opposite of the beautiful," it is its "counterweight" since it is no longer exactly a question of taste, given that it even flirts with horror, if not with disgust (*Anthropology,* 346). It is this relation between the beautiful and the sublime that, some thirty years after the 1764 *Observations,* the Third Critique will make more precise in more general terms and following a more formal argumentation.

The sublime, writes Kant, essentially shares the characteristics he had previously outlined in the "Analytic of the Beautiful":

> The beautiful coincides with the sublime in that both please for themselves. And further in that both presuppose neither a judgment of sense nor a logically determining judgment. . . . Consequently the satisfaction does not depend on a sensation, like that in the agreeable, nor on a determinate concept, like the satisfaction in the good. (*Critique of the Power of Judgment,* §23, 128)

In addition, if "both sorts of judgment are also *singular,*" if they are subjective, they are both essentially borne by the movement of universalization that is their very structure: They "profess to be universally valid in regard to every subject [*in Ansehung jedes Subjekts*], although they lay claim merely to the feeling of pleasure and not to any cognition of the object" (128).

After having recalled these general common characteristics, "The Analytic of the Sublime" quickly accentuates its differences from the beautiful. For Kant, beauty is thus related to the object's *form* whereas the sublime can emerge just as well—and perhaps even better—when faced with a *formless* object. And the satisfaction given by the beautiful goes hand in hand with the representation of *quality,* whereas that given by the sublime—and we will come back to this—implies *quantity.* But above all:

> Also the latter pleasure is very different in kind from the former, in that the former (the beautiful) directly brings with it a

feeling of the promotion of life, and hence is compatible with charms and an imagination at play, while the latter (the feeling of the sublime) is a pleasure that arises only indirectly, being generated, namely, by the feeling of a momentary inhibition of the vital powers and the immediately following and all the more powerful outpouring of them; hence as an emotion it seems to be not play but something serious in the activity of the imagination. Hence it is also incompatible with charms, and, since the mind is not merely attracted by the object, but is also always reciprocally repelled by it, the satisfaction in the sublime does not so much contain positive pleasure as it does admiration or respect, i.e., it deserves to be called negative pleasure. (*Critique of the Power of Judgment*, 128–29)

With the sublime, then, the game is off. Or if one does play, then it's a serious and grave game that is far from producing univocal pleasure. As the *Anthropology* will argue, this is why the sublime is no longer entirely a question of taste; and in the *Critique of the Power of Judgment*, its theory is considered "a mere appendix to the aesthetic judging" (130).

A mere appendix (*blossen Anhang*)? It is nonetheless in this apparently secondary supplement that we may find an opening to the veritable stakes of the question of the point of view in aesthetic judgment in general. For in the experience of the sublime, it is no longer merely a question, as it was with the beautiful, of a possible universalization of the judging subject's point of view. It is no longer merely a question of going from a singular point of view to that of each and every one (*jedermann*); it is rather a matter of the very condition of that universalization, of what might make it possible or impossible, of what might give it its chances or what could radically threaten it: In effect, the passage to universality presupposes that the particular or individual point of view be destabilized or unhooked—and as it happens, with the sublime, it is indeed the stability or the stance of a point of view that is going to start trembling. In this sense, and as we are getting ready to read, the loss of anchoring and destabilization of point of view produced in the sublime would rightfully precede any perspective of universalization as a way of announcing its fragile (and even impossible) possibility.

In short, the sublime is perhaps—within the gaze itself, in the stance of the *Standpunkt*—the moment of casting off, the raising of the telluric and earthly anchor onto which Schmitt, as we read, so wanted to *make us hold*.[17] In other words, the sublime would be the moment of takeoff, which, with its turbulence, *prepares* for the possibility of cosmopolitical expansion in the experience of the beautiful.

)) ((

So what then is the sublime?

Kant gives a minimal definition of it (if one can put it this way, given that it has to do with a certain maximum): "We call *sublime* that which is *absolutely great*" (*Critique of the Power of Judgment*, §25, 131). Or again, further on in the same paragraph: "The above explanation can also be expressed thus: *That is sublime that in comparison with which everything else is small*" (134).

Yet this comparison is no longer one of visible measure; it goes beyond sensible experience. As Kant explains, it engages a play with dimensions that makes all perspectives tremble in their relations to one another:

> Here one readily sees that nothing can be given in nature, however great it may be judged to be by us, which could not, considered in another relation [*in einem andern Verhältnisse betrachtet*], be diminished down to the infinitely small; and conversely, there is nothing so small which could not, in comparison with even smaller standards, be amplified for our imagination up to the magnitude of a world [*bis zu einer Weltgrösse*]. The telescope has given us rich material for the former observation, the microscope rich material for the latter. Thus nothing that can be an object of the senses is, considered on

this footing, to be called sublime [*nichts also, was Gegenstand der Sinnen sein kann, ist auf diesen Fuss betrachtet erhaben zu nennen*]. (*Critique of the Power of Judgment*, 134)

Worlds, Kant seems to be saying, and the dimensions of worlds (*Weltgrösse*), are infinitely relative: With a telescope, there is always a bigger world to judge another, smaller one; and seen through a microscope, the tiny can always be inflated to the size of a universe. But the experience of the sublime, while being the very experience of this dimensional vacillation, also signals toward another order, as if in the end it had to radicalize the comparative relativism of the plurality of worlds: It begins there where there is something incommensurable, in other words there where the possibility of having any standpoint (*Standpunkt*) trembles; there where, as the German literally says, one no longer has footing (*Fuss*), there where the ground or the very basis for *standing* (*se tenir*) somewhere in order to see is lacking. It's once there is no longer a point of view, once the point of view is no longer anchored to anything, that the sublime emerges on the horizon, unless, that is, the horizon of the sublime is without horizon, a radical trembling in the stance of the point of view where it is the act of seeing itself that *loses footing*.

In any case, the sublime thinks the point of view at the limits of sight by producing its constitutive instability. In a way, the sublime exposes the impossible point of view of the opening of any point of view. The sublime begins there where there is no more or not yet any point of view at all, no *Standpunkt*, no standpoint where one could stand to see, evaluate, measure, or judge. It is, in sum, the impossibility of *getting one's footing* somewhere to see (*auf diesen Fuss zu betrachten*).

)) ((

But what is this impossibility? And what does it mean? For us humans, us Earthlings, what is it a sign of?

If we follow Kant, it seems that it is quite precisely the sign of our humanity: in the end, this is that toward which "The Analytic of the Sublime" tends, and we need to read it further. In it, the sublime is in effect essentially tied to the horizonless horizon of the infinite: "Nature is thus sublime in those of its appearances the intuition of which brings with them the idea of its infinity. Now the latter cannot happen except through the inadequacy of even the greatest effort of our imagination in the estimation of the magnitude of an object" (*Critique of the Power of Judgment*, 138). In other words, "The infinite . . . is absolutely (not merely comparatively) great" (138). Yet the absolute magnitude of infinity insofar as we can think it implies "a faculty of the mind which surpasses every standard of sense," a suprasensible faculty, or reason. In the final analysis, the sublime is thus play between imagination and reason,[18] where imagination is constantly losing to the demands of reason. Imagination tries and does what it can in its confrontation with reason that is constantly prodding it to go further, for it to go all the way to the presentation of ideas themselves; but it is unable to and declares forfeit, leaving room for the elevation of mind that makes for the sublime: "The mind feels itself elevated . . . if . . . abandoning itself to the imagination and to a reason which . . . merely extends it, it nevertheless finds the entire power of the imagination inadequate to its ideas" (139–40).

Now, Kant's principal example for illustrating the insufficiency of the imagination that gives birth to the sense of the sublime is quite precisely that of an incommensurability that directly implies the cosmotheoretical vision of a plurality of worlds:

A tree that we estimate by the height of a man may serve as a standard for a mountain, and, if the latter were, say, a mile high, it could serve as the limit for the number that expresses the diameter of the earth, in order to make the latter intuitable; the diameter of the earth could serve as the unit for the planetary system so far as known to us, this for the Milky Way, and the immeasurable multitude of such Milky Way systems, called nebulae, which presumably constitute such a system among themselves in turn, does not allow us to expect any limits here. Now in the aesthetic judging of such an immeasurable whole, the sublime does not lie as much in the magnitude of the number as in the fact that as we progress we always arrive at ever greater units; the systematic division of the structure of the world contributes to this, . . . representing our imagination in all its boundlessness, and with it nature, as paling in significance beside the ideas of reason if it is supposed to provide a presentation adequate to them. (*Critique of the Power of Judgment,* 140)

Progressing from a mountain to the Milky Way and beyond, surveying human and earthly measures in order to multiply them to cosmic dimensions, imagination doesn't make it; it gives up and concedes its place to pure reason while its failure inspires a negative pleasure, an indirect or secondary satisfaction that is the sublime itself:

The feeling of the sublime is thus a feeling of displeasure from the inadequacy of the imagination in the aesthetic estimation of magnitude for the estimation by means of reason, and a pleasure that is thereby aroused at the same time from the correspondence of this very judgment of the inadequacy of the greatest sensible faculty in comparison with ideas of reason, insofar as striving for them is nevertheless a law for us. That is, it is a law (of reason) for us and part of our vocation to estimate everything great that nature contains as an object of the senses for us as small in comparison with ideas of reason. . . . Thus the inner perception of the inadequacy of any sensible standard for the estimation of magnitude by reason corresponds with reason's laws, and it is a displeasure that arouses the feeling of our supersensible vocation in us, in accordance with which it is purposive and thus a pleasure to find every standard of sensibility inadequate for the ideas of reason. . . .

Judgment itself . . . represents merely the subjective play of the powers of the mind (imagination and reason) as harmonious even in their contrast. (*Critique of the Power of Judgment*, 141–42, translation slightly modified)

At bottom, the sublime is the experience of the unimaginable, given that the insufficiency of imagination for *us*, that is to say for *us humans*, is a law. And this is why in the sublime, we take pleasure—a certainly paradoxical pleasure—in our constitutive failure.

In the experience of the sublime, there is thus indeed an implicit comparison (others, wholly other others, might be endowed with a form of imagination equal to their reason). Yet this lack of ours that is thus revealed to us can be experienced only in the unpresentability of any comparative term. In this sense, the sublime would be the translation in advance, in terms of aesthetic judgment, of the phrase from the *Anthropology* that we have read and reread: The solution to the problem of the characterization of humanity—in other words, in this case, mutatis mutandis, the sense of our human condition—implies "the comparison of two *species* of rational being, but experience does not offer us this possibility."

The sublime also *relies on* and *clings to* [*tient à*] the impossible possibility of the absolutely other.

)) ((

Such is the first form of the sublime, which Kant calls the "mathematical" (*Critique of the Power of Judgment*, 131) sublime. He compares it to a second form, the "dynamical" sublime that is related to "power" more than to the idea of infinity.

Bold, overhanging, as it were threatening cliffs, thunder clouds towering up into the heavens, bringing with them flashes of lightning and crashes of thunder, volcanoes with their all-destroying violence, hurricanes with the devastation they leave behind, the boundless ocean set into a rage, a lofty waterfall on a mighty river, etc., make our capacity to resist into an insignificant trifle in comparison with their power. But the sight of them only becomes all the more attractive the more fearful it is, as long as we find ourselves in safety, and we gladly call these objects sublime because they elevate the strength of our soul above its usual level, and allow us to discover within ourselves a capacity for resistance of quite another kind, which gives us the courage to measure ourselves against the apparent all-powerfulness of nature. (*Critique of the Power of Judgment*, 144–45)

In this second form of the sublime, the trembling of the ground or base that founds the point of view (*Standpunkt*) becomes more violent than ever before since it is the destruction of our being which, even if only in our imagination, is announced before mixing in with the ambiguous satisfaction we feel. But this is only to reveal and unveil our humanity (*Menschheit*) thanks to a judgment we finally carry out *on ourselves*, as humans overwhelmed by what radically surpasses us. As Kant writes:

The irresistibility of [the] power [of nature] certainly makes us, considered as natural beings, recognize our physical powerlessness, but at the same time it reveals a capacity for judging *ourselves* [emphasis mine] as independent of it and a superiority over nature on which is grounded a self-preservation of quite another kind than that which can be threatened and endangered by nature outside us, whereby the *humanity in our person* [my emphasis once again: *die Menschheit in unserer Person*] remains undemeaned even though the human being must submit to that dominion. (*Critique of the Power of Judgment*, 145)

It is in the play between reason and imagination, where "the mind can make palpable to itself the sublimity of its own vocation even over nature" (145) that aesthetic judgment looks back in a judgment *on ourselves*, to signify our humanity for us, to extract it from the very experience of our insufficiency. This is the humanity the *Anthropology* will say, as we've seen, cannot be conceptualized as a race without an (impossible) comparison with reasonable beings from other planets. Here, this humanity is thus experienced without any reference to a *determined* comparative. It is experienced, perhaps even incorporated, according to a *comparison with one sole term* and on the basis of the trembling lack of the point of view it needs.

In sum, if what is at stake with the beautiful is the expansion of the individual point of view to the universal point of view of humanity, the sublime exposes the very condition of the human as human, in other words as a being who can only understand itself as such from a cosmopolitical or cosmotheoretical perspective, from the unattainable point of view of the wholly other.

Incipit Fantascientia: They Are Already Here

Extraterrestrials are thus here among us humans and Earthlings. They are here, but they remain impossible to find; we know nothing about them.

They are here—and they have probably always been here—since they work their way through the very texture of what is offered by our senses to judgment. They are *already here*, at the heart of the perceptible weft, even before it becomes a question of their possible arrival, even before we imagine them as potential invaders from far away at the other end of the universe.

Yet they are not here as a presence: neither simply present nor simply absent, their being-there, we could say, is a *being-out-there, down here*.[19]

This is why science fiction will have always already begun. *Incipit fantascientia.*

)) ((

We can see or glimpse those who have forever accompanied us as our shadows in a futurist comedy whose screenplay could, in many ways, have been written by Kant. In *Men in Black*, directed by Barry Sonnenfeld and released in 1997, two strange men in black have been given the task of maintaining order for a *cosmic politics*, as Kay (Tommy Lee Jones) explains to Jay (Will Smith):

> Back in the mid-fifties, the government [of the United States] started a little underfunded agency with the simple and laughable purpose of making contact with a race not of this planet. . . . Everybody thought the agency was a joke. Except the aliens. They made contact on March 2nd, 1961, outside New York City. . . . They were intergalactic refugees with a simple request. Let us use the earth as an apolitical zone for creatures without a planet. . . . We agreed. So we masked all evidence of their landing. . . . More nonhumans arrive every year. They live among us, in secret. . . . Most aliens are decent enough, just trying to make a living. . . . Humans, for the most part, don't have a clue. Don't want one, either. They're happy.

Jay, who is wondering if he should agree to join the agency in question or not—which would imply giving up his name, his identity, in short, everything that made him a human—is dubious. He is surprised that this extraterrestrial presence is kept secret. "People," he says to Kay, meaning Earthlings, "can handle" this knowledge; they are responsible enough, "smart" enough to deal with it. Kay's response to him:

> A person is smart. People are dumb, panicky, dangerous animals and you know it. Fifteen hundred years ago everybody knew the Earth was the center of the universe. Five hundred years ago, everybody knew the Earth was flat, and fifteen minutes ago, you knew that humans were alone on this planet. Imagine what you'll know tomorrow.

Extraterrestrial presence on earth and the necessity of keeping it secret, even of regulating it through the ad hoc police authority of men dressed in black, are related to stakes that are thus liter-ally cosmopolitical. Not only in the sense Kant generally gives the term in order to designate anything that concerns the citizens of the earthly world that we are, but also in the sense that Kant must presuppose here and there when he gestures toward the population of the cosmos and the plurality of inhabited worlds. As if earthly political questions—interstate conflicts and the per-spectives of peace that are distributed not to persons taken indi-vidually but, to take up Kay's words again, to those dumb, panicky, dangerous animals that people in society are—as if these questions that agitate us inhabitants of Earth needed, in order to be thought, to be formulated against the horizon of a politics understood in its cosmic dimensions, grappling with interstellar refugees and intergalactic strategies.

Distraught, incarnating the disorientation of the earthly point of view as it considers this horizon whose universality is both too vast and nonetheless necessary, Jay asks about the conditions of his possible employment by the agency. What will he have to do, what will he have to sacrifice to be a part of a cosmopolitan police force regulating and overseeing the movement of inter-planetary immigrants?

Kay's answer: "The catch is you will sever every human con-tact. Nobody will ever know you exist anywhere. Ever."

In effect, as the voice-over embodying the authority of this pla-celess law says, Jay will have to renounce all marks that might characterize him. His name will be no more than an initial (J), he will have to wear only black, to conform to the identity given to him, eat what he is told to eat, live where he is instructed to live. And Jay's entering into cosmopolitan anonymity continues against a backdrop of digital screens that show the erasure of his finger prints and all other data.

> You will have no identifying marks of any kind. . . . Your entire image is carefully crafted to leave no lasting memory whatso-ever with anyone you encounter. You're a rumor. . . . You don't

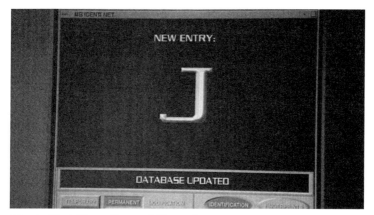

Men in Black (Barry Sonnenfeld, 1997)

Men in Black (Barry Sonnenfeld, 1997)

exist; you were never even born. Anonymity is your name. Silence your native tongue. You are no longer part of "the system." We're above the system. Over it. Beyond it. We're "them." We're "they." We are the Men in Black.

This sequence of an initiatory rite that closes with an allusion to the title of the movie thus makes of Jay a being it is impossible to characterize, like the human race itself as a race, according to Kant's *Anthropology*. Jay becomes an Earthling having lost any mark that could determine him as such, the representative of an undefined species, with no affiliation whatsoever. This seems to be the condition for taking oneself beyond the "system," beyond the territoriality of a planetary anchoring, beyond the telluric ground or base as a way of gaining a properly universal point of view. The cosmic cosmopolitics of the police of men in black is only possible at the price of absolute indetermination.

But this also means at the risk of becoming other. For what are the men in black, these Earthlings in the process of losing any attachment to the Earth? They define themselves—or undefine themselves—as other: *they, them.* They present themselves, by the very movement that makes them absent, as "the others," even as the absolutely other. At bottom, they are already extraterrestrials and probably much more so than the aliens they are supposed to police: The intergalactic refugees take on human and very human forms—they could not be any more hominoid—while the cosmopolitan agency that regulates their right to asylum and their "universal hospitality"[20] on Earth is composed of Earthlings in the midst of mutating toward total indeterminacy.

)) ((

It is only by thus indetermining himself that Jay, Kay, and the other men in black can accomplish their mission over the course of which they are often brought to make the extraterrestrials appear for what they are. They regularly force them to leave their borrowed human forms. For the aliens do not willfully show themselves as such in the eyes of men, whose appearance they take on, putting it on like a piece of clothing.

It thus sometimes happens that the men in black reveal the veritable hidden physiognomy of the intergalactic refugees. And what is this true nature covered up by the makeup of their human appearances? What of the cosmic essence of these inhabitants of the cosmos becomes manifest when one forcefully takes off the cosmetic finery that makes them resemble us? What is there? What is left when the sensible's makeup has thus been removed? Nothing, nothing but an ultrathin envelope: This is all that is left of the aliens when the men in black lay them bare by seizing them, X-raying them with a gaze that pierces through the thickness of their flesh.

When the cosmocops force them to unmask themselves, it in effect sometimes happens that the extraterrestrial creatures become uncontrollable. The men in black are then forced to use their weapons—pistols that emit a luminous beam that rips through the image; they have to fire, "to shoot," as they say in English. But a "shot" is not only a gunshot. In the lexicon of photography or film, it also refers to a snapshot, an optical grasp or catch. The eye's *nomos*, we might say with a mind to Schmitt's appropriations, a visual *Nahme*. And what is one thus taking, what is one seizing in the luminous lightning bolts launched by Jay or Kay? Under the cops' fire, the aliens, already unmasked or having exchanged their human guise (their anthropomorphic *cosmos* or *mundus*)[21] for their veritable appearance, are reduced, *in fine*, to a kind of transparent glue, a—barely colored—translucent membrane that slightly sticks to things and beings. Behind their stratified phenomenality, there is (nothing but) this *film* they leave behind; in the final analysis, after all the layers have been stripped away, there is *the very film of appearances* that seems to have melted.

It remains the case that, if any eventual witnesses happened to be there by chance and see the secret operations of the men in black, the latter have to then erase the sensible traces that might have been engraved in human memories: As members of humanity, we must know nothing about the presence of the aliens; we must not remember what we have seen. This is why the agents use a neurolyzer, a small apparatus that emits a red light to sweep away the mnemonic traces left by the extraterrestrials. To clean up the sensible.

Men in Black (Barry Sonnenfeld, 1997)

Men in Black (Barry Sonnenfeld, 1997)

For the sensible—*this* particular, very sensitive sensible—must not be inscribed or written into the archive of the collective memory of the ordinary humans that we are. The men in black thus control and distribute the visible according to a segregation of and within perception whose responsibility is theirs: What thus also befalls them is what Jacques Rancière has called a *distribution of the sensible*, at stake in a politics that regulates "what

Men in Black (Barry Sonnenfeld, 1997)

one sees and what one can say about it," defining "who has the competence to see and the qualification to say."[22]

But the politics of Jay, Kay, and the other cops assigned to overseeing the universe's immigrants is above all a cosmopolitics. Confronted with "intergalactic refugees," it operates against the backdrop of an appropriation and distribution of cosmic space and is indissociable from what we have followed Schmitt in calling a *nomos* of the cosmos, which is immediately declined into an appropriation and division of what is given to be seen, immediately translated into a cosmopolice of the visible.[23] What the men in black thus lead us to think is a veritable *cosmonomics of the sensible*, before or beyond what Rancière describes as its merely anthropogeocentric division.

This cosmopolitan division is remarked and retraced on the screen, in the film, when Jay and Kay put on black glasses to "neurolyze" their compatriots on Earth. Of course, they do so to protect themselves, to place between their gaze and that of others a reflective surface that shelters them from the amnesia they inflict. Yet this screen placed in front of their eyes is fundamentally the same one that allows us spectators to see with them what humans should not see. This screen is a gap that splits the gaze from itself, dividing it—distributing it, yes, yet this distribution *down here* of the shares of the visible takes place on the basis of humanity's indefinition (which is also its de-earthing, its unanchoring) and its unpresentable comparison with an utterly other that is already there (with these earthlinged extraterrestrials whose alterity determines in turn "every perceptible criteria," as Kant would say).

With the men in black, what happens to us is thus both extremely unusual and extremely banal. We get a glimpse of the fiction of what we should not be able to see. We briefly see what divides our gaze, we half-open our eyes onto what, in these eyes, regulates the opening or the closing: We oscillate between, on the one hand, the identification that consigns us to the point of view of ordinary humans kept apart from what must remain invisible to humans, and, on the other hand, the fictive access to *the point of view of this point of view*, according to an overlooking perspective that shows us its structure.

"Above the system," as the voice-over gravely declared, "we are them."

And we are *off, off we go*, unanchored, unstuck from the Earth, from the ground or foundation of our gaze (from the telluric *Standpunkt* that, for Schmitt, seemed to have to ensure us of a stable *Blickpunkt*). But this takeoff does not take us to any outside: It is itself, like a film, stuck to appearances.

It weaves and warps them.

)) ((

As for the men in black reduced to the anonymity of an initial, who, when it comes down to it, are they? Who are those who, before its anthropogeocentric division, are already policing the *cosmopartition* of the sensible?

If, as Sigfried Kracauer would have it, the traditional detective of the crime novel is Kantian reason in action and at work,[24] who is it that these new cosmotheoretical detectives embody in their confrontation with universal criminality and migration?

They are probably not merely investigating something beyond reason but rather something that, beyond *our* reason, gives it its philosofictive reason.

Probably. But in that case one must also add that fiction—or even better: *effiction*—is not in opposition to reason and its enlightenment: Nothing is more rational and reasonable in effect than philosofiction when it begins to investigate, as it does in Kant, as it does in Kay, a nonhuman and nonearthly *ratio*. It is then under way on its journey toward a reason yet to come, one that is becoming.[25]

CHAPTER 4   *Weightless: The Archimedean Point of the Sensible*

"When you look at the stars at night, you get the impression deep down in your gut that you don't know who you are, that you know more about what is going on out there than what is going on down here," says Jay to Kay in the second part of *Men in Black (MIIB)*.[1]

Maybe, after all, he's right.

Or rather, as you suggested to me when you came to meet me one night: Our time and our orientation in space, here, on our Earth, is widely determined by what is weaving its way through the cosmos. You were waiting for the bus, you told me, and you were impatiently looking at the indication of how long you'd have to wait, which wavered, until a message notified you and the other bus riders that the geo-satellite system for following traffic was momentarily out of order. "Have you ever thought about it?" you asked me with surprise. "In our lived experience of time passing and moving through space, we depend on data that come back to us from what we emit beyond the earth's atmosphere."

"It's true," I thought while I listened to you, "you've come back from far away. Your little feet on this Earth, as that other guy would say, are inhabited by a giant's leaps."

)) ((

Of course, our movements *down here*, our perceptions, our access to the sensible are increasingly guided by devices that orient us from *out there*, from what Hannah Arendt described as an "Archimedean point" that moves away from our planet and on the basis of which we act on it.[2] But, as we have seen by stalking extraterrestrials all the way into the corners of the Kantian sublime, the cosmonomic distribution of what is offered to our senses hasn't waited for recent geo-satellite technologies to settle into place. The sensible *is distributed* [*se partage*] from the heart of aesthetic experience, which is for that very reason—because it is a question of distribution—immediately political.[3] Or rather cosmopolitical since the opening of each human point of view immediately implies the philosofiction of the extraterrestrial wholly other. This is so much the case that one could speak, as we have done following Carl Schmitt, of a *nomos of the sensible*, inscribing the stakes of its division in a cosmic perspective, which, far from being futurist or utopian, far from simply being a matter of science fiction in the habitual and restricted sense of this term, is at work within each of our gazes on the world.[4]

This cosmotheoretical and cosmopolitical gap that carves out our points of view, running through them like the fold of the difference that makes them possible, would thus be the philosofictive extra-earthliness of the wholly other, imprinting itself in the depths of the sensible. This *Archimedean point of the sensible* where its *nomos* and geopolitics are traced and retraced— Kant is no doubt the first to have glimpsed it and indicated it in between the lines of his writing—Kant, who, as we were saying, is also the last representative of a long pluriworldist philosophical tradition.

The last one?

When others, after Kant, have evoked diverse figures of extra-earthliness in their discourse, it was most often in a sporadic and fugitive way. There is nonetheless one exception that must be mentioned here and that would itself merit a very careful reading: I am thinking of a surprising manuscript by Husserl that was long unpublished, written in May 1934 and devoted to "a reversal of Copernican doctrine."[5]

Imagining "flying arks" and "humanities"—in the plural—transported into the stars ("Originary Ark," 127), Husserl would seem here almost to share Carl Schmitt's interest in science fiction.[6] Whatever the case may be, several years after the Schmittean formulation that held our attention for quite a while ("Humanity as such . . . has no enemy, at least not on this planet"), Husserl carries out a thought experiment and engages in philosofictive variations that bring him to consider the existence of more than one Earth (e.g. "two earths" [125]) as well as—supreme and apocalyptic philosofiction—the total destruction of our globe ("It is possible that entropy will put an end to all life on earth, or that celestial bodies will crash into the earth, etc.," 131). And here too, as with Schmitt, the maritime paradigm and its naval or nautical vocabulary, allows us to feel the possible extra-earthly extension of the "house" and "home":

> If I am born a sailor's child, then a part of my development has taken place on the ship. But the ship . . . would itself be my "earth," my homeland. But my parents are not then primordially at home on the ship; they still have the old home, another primordial homeland. . . . Let us now consider the stars . . . as mere "airships," "spaceships" of the earth, by departing from it and then returning back to it, inhabited and guided by human beings who . . . have made their home on the earth-ground as their ark. . . . The earth-ark itself . . . is not . . . a star among other stars. Only when we think of our stars as secondary arks with their eventual humanities, etc., only when we figure ourselves as transplanted there among these humanities, perhaps flying there, is it otherwise. Then it is like children born on ships, but with some differences. ("Originary Ark," 126–27)

Like Schmitt, and even more than Schmitt, Husserl goes a long way with the unearthing hypotheses of a navigator floating in weightlessness. Yet at the end of his trajectory, he, too, reaffirms the original and founding character of earthly ground. Despite the audacity of his considerations on interplanetary flight—which bring him almost literally to anticipate the gripping Schmittean formulation, "To make of the planet we inhabit, to make of the Earth itself, a spaceship"—they do not in the end change anything at all of the uniqueness and centrality of our planet Earth. And the Robinsonian philosofiction of the deserted island, which crosses through the sidelines of this stunning and sidereal [*sidérale et sidérante*] scene, can only confirm the *geocentrism* of these pages:

> I could just as well think of myself as transplanted to the moon. Why should I not think of the moon as something like an earth, as therefore something like a land for animal habitation? Indeed, I can very well think of myself as a bird flying off from the earth to a body that lies far away, or as a pilot of an airplane that flies off and lands there. Certainly, I can conceive of human beings and animals already being there. But I ask, perhaps, "how have they gotten there?"—then, just as similarly in the case of a new island where cuneiform writing is found, I ask: How did the people in question come there? All animals, all living beings, all beings whatsoever, have ontic being only on the basis of my constitutive genesis and this has "earthly" precedence. Indeed, a fragment of the earth (like an ice floe) may have become detached, and that has made a particular historicity possible. But that does not mean that the moon or Venus could not just as well be conceived as primordial homes . . . and that does not mean that the being of the earth is precisely only a fact [meaning a mere contingent fact] for me and our terrestrial humanity. There is only one humanity and one earth—all the fragments which are or have been separated from it belong to it. But if this is the case, need we say with Galileo: *eppur si muove?*. . . It is certainly not so that it rests in space . . . but rather, as we tried to show above, the

earth is the ark which makes possible in the first place the sense of all motion and all rest as mode of one motion. ("Originary Ark," 130, translation modified)

Wherever we go, wherever we fly, Husserl's transcendental Earth comes with us and even precedes us as a "carnal flight-vessel" (*Leib-Flugschiff*) (125).

This movement ultimately conceived of *on the basis of the Earth*, this re-earthing gesture is one which Kant, as we've seen, also did not escape. But what gave his thinking its particular reach, all at once cosmotheoretical, cosmopolitical and cosmetic, is the fact that extra-earthliness was constantly *returning* in order to destabilize *in spite of it all* the earthly anchoring of the subjects that we are.

This is also the impression we get from these pages of Husserl. They may well repatriate us back to Earth in the last and original instance; they may well situate our originary home there as transcendental subjects, their undeniable textual effect, their *effiction* in spite of themselves is to make the earthly bedrock tremble.

And yet for Kant as for Husserl, as it was in all the preceding pages, an opposition remains between *down here* and *out there*. This is no doubt as it should be since, until further notice, we spend the vast majority of our time on Earth. And for the time that still remains for us to spend here as humans, even as we philosofictively allow ourselves from time to time to announce its end,[7] in this meantime that assigns us to the finitude of the bedrock that carries the finite beings we are, what we must think is a cosmopolitics of the sensible ever more increasingly turned away from its telluric, earthly anchoring toward and by a movement that implicates the extra-earthliness of a cosmos that is thus anything but a mere outside.

)) ((

"One small step for a man, one giant leap for mankind," declared Neil Armstrong when he put his foot down onto lunar ground in 1969.

We, too, have taken a few steps and made a few leaps since we launched this philosofictive adventure that will have taken us through quite a few spaces of thought. We leaped in ways that defied the laws of gravity in reason: We went from space tourism to Carl Schmitt, from Schmitt to Kant, from Kant to film—and back, from film or TV series to Kant, from Kant to contemporary geopolitics and to the most urgent planetary or ecological questions. . . . All of this was done without the least apparent concern for a particular kind of gravity, for a certain *weight of thought* [*pesée de la pensée*]. For if thinking and weighing, *penser* and *peser*, have a common origin in Romance languages (the Latin *pensare* is the intensive form of *pendere*),[8] the weight of a thought, its load, should reside at least in the way it ballasts its objects, the way it does not allow them to fly away or disappear, forces them to *gravitate* around what it interrogates by forming a regulated constellation.

Is it then mere *lightness* that brought us to make these leaps? Is it not much more an undeniable *proximity* that made us jump from one planet or sphere to another (from Kant to film, from Schmitt to science fiction . . .), like the protagonist in one of Calvino's tales who, at a time when the Moon was thought to be much closer to the Earth than it is today, is constantly spanning the distance separating the two stars, his major project being to move from the one to the other without respite?[9]

If we suppose, for example, that in this case Kant is the Earth and cinema is the Moon (though it could also be the other way around, a truly weighty thinking should certainly justify this casting), it does indeed seem difficult while staying close to the Königsberg thinker's texts, on Earth, not to exclaim like that other character from Calvino's book, perched on top of a ladder and getting dangerously close to the satellite, "Stop! Stop! I'm going to bang my head!"

Once we attempt, with Kant, to think what is called a point of view, our head, as we have constantly had occasion to verify, is in the stars: Reading Kant with a certain eye, we are structurally on the Moon, already, in other words, at the movies.

Film is in effect perhaps above all an affair of point of view. It's an incredible experience of point of view and its variations, shifts, and extensions; it is the always singular invention of a wholly other point of view, of a point of view beyond points of view that would be the very limit, constantly retraced, of any possible point of view. And this is why, beyond the whims of fashion and the choices that govern a screenplay's writing, beyond even filmic genres, cinema has always had something telescopic about it, even in its close-ups: It is always stretched toward that distance, however close it may be, from which seeing is constituted into a point of view while becoming unstable, vacillating and losing its footing.[10]

If Eisenstein was able to say that "Diderot spoke of cinema,"[11] one could paraphrase this scandalous anachronism and affirm that Kant analyzed in advance the states that we, Earthlings that we are, live out in front of screens populated with extraterrestrials. Yes, with Kant just like at the movies, inhabitants of other worlds besiege us. But not like invaders that come from outside: rather, like those who have always already been there, inhabiting our point of view with their extraneity that makes it possible.

If this is true, it would then be necessary to write, with Kant, following the Kantian gaze in its constitution from the point of view of the wholly other, a genealogy of science fiction in film. But that would be another book entirely. A book I've dreamed of, a real book, perhaps, of philosofiction. Here, I'll content myself with simply imagining its beginnings.

)) ((

Incipit fantascientia, once again.

In 1902, Georges Méliès directed his *Trip to the Moon*. Astronomers have gathered for an extraordinary meeting and attend the conference of a great professor (Barbenfouillis) who is presenting his project: sending people to the Moon in a bullet shot by a giant cannon. They protest, incredulous, but five of them, the bravest ones, agree to participate in this crazy enterprise. The day of departure finally arrives. The bullet flies toward the Moon that awaits it and that, little by little, as it gets closer and closer, looks like a face made up in white, with eyes, a mouth, a nose.[12] All of a sudden, while the camera shows this human face of the lunar star, the bullet comes up and gets stuck in her right eye. The Moon's eye is poked out. White like a cream tart or a screen within the screen, the moon was watching us, but she doesn't see very well any more, having just received an emission from earth right in her eyes. She's half-blind.

The scene changes. In a kind of cosmicomic countershot, the Moon's face as seen from the Earth makes way for the image of the five astronomers landing on lunar ground. They emerge from the bullet and, waving their hats, see the earth lit up from afar before wrapping themselves in blankets to go to sleep while a comet passes over their heads. Stars light up during their sleep and they, too, have faces. They are awakened by a shower of stellar dust and get up to venture inland, into a cave invaded with

Le Voyage dans la Lune (Georges Méliès, 1902)

Le Voyage dans la Lune (Georges Méliès, 1902)

giant mushrooms. This is where the Selenites appear, the inhabitants of the Moon who capture the five astronomers. But they manage to escape: They make their way back to their bullet, which seems to be hanging right at the edge of a cliff and, pulled in by earthly gravity, they allow themselves to fall into the ocean, where a paddle boat tows them for the festivities and honors awaiting them at the conclusion of this fantastic voyage.

In this ultimately banal story, in this tale inspired by Jules Verne (*From the Earth to the Moon*, 1865) that turns the Selenites into entirely predictable anthropomorphic savages, why does Méliès make this gesture, now engraved into the visual memory of film history as a veritable icon, of putting the Moon's eye out? Of course, this is in part inherited from farce, the cream tart slapped in the face, the circus comedy whose tradition of clowning is thus put into film. But the gesture goes far beyond its eventual precedents: With its whiteness given eyes, the Moon, as we were saying, is a kind of screen within the screen. It's the screen showed on the screen, the screen that appears on the screen as the very apparatus [*dispositif*] of sight. And thus ripping the screen [*crever l'écran*] means piercing it with a gaze sent toward its galactic outside, toward a cosmotheoretical perspective that is like the horizon without horizon of any possible point of view. Only this perspective, lodged somewhere beyond the screen, would allow us to appear to ourselves, to see ourselves as an earthly species with looks.

But this lunar point of view is barred to us; it is prohibited. We rip it in the very experience we attempt to have of it. Or rather, and more precisely, we rip it halfway; we only put one eye out while the other, blinking and trying to see as best it can, accords us, as if in a blink and for no longer than an instant before getting lost, a glimpse of ourselves as seers [*une entrevue sur nous-mêmes en tant que voyants*].

This is the impossible interplanetary effect of the shot and countershot of which Kant also spoke. Yet the infinite space, the interstellar space implied in such a (counter)shot, in a way that is both improbable and necessary, this space is not only that of journeys to the Moon, or even of cosmic journeys. As Méliès's film shows no doubt in spite of itself, this space is already that of every intraterrestrial experience. It's the space that opens within every human or earthling point of view in order to make possible a point of view as such: If, in Méliès's science fiction as in so many others, including those of Fontenelle or Kant, the Moon and the other planets appear as a projection of our geocentric geography, as a cosmotheoretical enlargement of our human, all too human, perspectives, this is not, or not only, because the other cannot be given any figure other than in the characteristics of the same; it is also because the intersidereal distance summoned by these stories is already lodged in what is smallest in each terrestrial gaze.

If in the end Méliès's astronomers seem to have never left the Earth, if they find the world here without much change in the world out there, this is because they have only made the Earth itself distant from itself, projected to an interplanetary distance from itself. As if this cosmic adventure already actually took place every time we look.

As if telescopy were already lodged in the myopic microscopy of each gaze in order to make it possible as a point of view: there where some vision blinks, starting to peep through while hesitating to be [*à poindre tout en menaçant de n'être point*].

)) ((

Incipit fantascientia, again and again.

In the prologue to Steven Spielberg's adaptation of *War of the Worlds* (2005), a voice-over, serious and as sententious as always, accompanies the first images, those of the Earth that seems at first to be contained in a drop of water that's fallen onto a green leaf. The voice warns us: "No one would have believed in the early years of the twenty-first century that our world was being watched by intelligences greater than our own."

Even if Spielberg gives it a new little ecological twist that Al Gore would not deny, the story is well known and has become banal and cliché: Extraterrestrials, having exhausted their home's resources, are going to attack this world and exploit it until it is destroyed.

Buried underground for millennia, they were, however, already here, and they now awaken to cause massive destruction. Among the few survivors being chased by immense tripods with tentacles, Ray (Tom Cruise) and his daughter Rachel (Dakota Fanning) have burrowed into a basement in order not to be seen and to escape death. All of a sudden a tentacle climbs down into their refuge, slowly, scrutinizing every corner to make sure no Earthlings are hiding in them. Seen in a close-up, the end of the mobile arm that serves as the creature's eye looks like a camera lens. It is a glass surface on which surrounding space is reflected. This is a detail Spielberg took from the first film adaptation of the novel done by Byron Haskin in 1953, for Herbert George Wells only speaks of "a long metallic snake of tentacle [that] came feeling slowly through the hole."[13]

War of the Worlds (Byron Haskin, 1953)

In Spielberg's adaptation, then, the camera thanks to which we spectators see, the camera that shows us the film's world and a quasi lens on the tentacle, this camera seems to be, in this sequence where we hold our breath, faced with a double of itself. The extraterrestrial eye is the filmic eye itself, filmed in the film. Like the camera's eye, it is mobile, can go into any space, into the slightest interstices of this underground basement. In short, we Earthlings, we who, like Ray and Rachel, look at this eye coming to find us even underground and "penetrating, in the most intensive way, into reality,"[14] we find ourselves confronted with our own cinematographic gaze, so near, so troubling and yet infinitely faraway.

In the few yards that separate Ray and Rachel's eyes from this inhuman eye is lodged all the abyssal distance that exists between our gaze and itself: a necessary distance that must inhabit human and earthly vision for it to be able to adopt a point of view, this particular point of view instead of another. For there is always more than one point of view, and this plurality besieges or haunts each singular point of view by making it possible as such.

Ray and Rachel, the film's characters being filmed by the camera that is our eye, attempt to flee this other camera, this other eye that is hunting them. We see them, they who live only through and for our gaze; we see them as if they were attempting to remove themselves from what nonetheless makes them

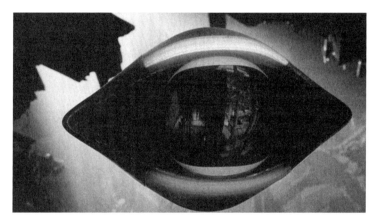

War of the Worlds (Steven Spielberg, 2005)

War of the Worlds (Steven Spielberg, 2005)

possible as filmic beings. And once the unfortunate fall of an object attracts the attention of the ocular tentacle, Ray hides with his daughter behind a mirror: The extraterrestrial quasi camera is reflected in it; it sees itself there and gazes at its reflection, just as it itself reflected the image of our gaze back to us. Face to face, only a few centimeters apart, the eye from elsewhere and the Earthlings burrowed in the basement are nonetheless separated by the infinite distance between a gaze and its double in the mirror. They are distanced by the cosmotheoretical distance that inhabits every gaze and separates it from itself to constitute it as a point of view.

This is a gripping way to show us that we, we Earthlings, we humans, we see (ourselves) only under the condition of the other's gaze; we have a point of view only if we allow it to be haunted by the wholly other. Which is faraway, at an infinite distance in the light-years that distance it from us, and yet so close, stuck to our point of view to the point that it redoubles it.

This wholly other is thus the gap of seeing within seeing that alone allows for something like a point of view. It's the intergalactic distance that is lodged in the most intimate or minute angle, between eye and eye.

This is why, when we open our eye, notably and significantly at the movies, our point of view is structurally besieged by those extraterrestrials that make it possible, before they even appear on the screen or in real life.

They are already there; they besiege our point of view so that it might be ours. They keep the siege that a point of view sustains and thanks to which it holds.

So much so that the war of the worlds has already taken place, every time we look.

Postface: **What's Left of Cosmopolitanism?**

> Where have we received the figure of cosmopolitanism from? And what is happening to it? As for the figure of the citizen of the world, we do not know if it has a future in store for it.
>
> —Jacques Derrida, *On Cosmopolitanism and Forgiveness*

These are the first words of a pamphlet whose original French title can be translated as "Cosmopolitans of All Lands, Yet Another Effort!"[1] For this certainly is a pamphlet, yes, at least in the somewhat archaic sense the term currently has in French, in other words, quite simply a piece of writing consisting of a very small number of pages. And this very little book—maybe the shortest of all those Derrida published—ends by citing "a certain idea of cosmopolitanism, *an other,* [that] has not yet arrived, perhaps," or that "has perhaps not yet been recognized" (Derrida, *On Cosmopolitanism,* 23).

I am constantly reciting and repeating the abrupt juxtaposition of that beginning and this end. On the one hand, this thing or this cause named cosmopolitanism has perhaps not yet arrived or has perhaps gone unnoticed. But on the other hand, one does not know or no longer knows if it still has a future.

What then might be left of cosmopolitanism?

Perhaps nothing, if it had to be left as the history of its devaluation has given it over to us.

Yet perhaps it is entirely left to come, like that *other* cosmopolitanism for which Derrida, more than anyone else, will have advocated.

)) ((

Let us start then by lending an ear to the injunction of the title, with the imperative that attends its exclamation point: "Cosmopolitans of All Lands, Yet Another Effort!"

The title is something of a monstrous hybrid that plays at deforming the overly famous concluding sentence of Marx's *Communist Manifesto* ("Workers of all lands, unite!") by coupling it with the title of the "brochure" inserted into the fifth dialogue of *Philosophy in the Bedroom* by the marquis de Sade ("Yet Another Effort, Frenchmen, If You Would Become Republicans").

Such a rewriting is no small matter. Especially when one considers that Marx's quip (*Proletarier aller Länder*) is replaced with the name of those cosmopolitans that the author of the *Communist Manifesto* had a tendency to see as the instruments of globalized capitalist domination. One need only be reminded, for example, that in *The Civil War in France* (1871), Marx speaks of the "cosmopolitan orgies" of "financial speculation" (*der Finanzschwindel feierte kosmopolitische Orgien*) or else of "capital's cosmopolitan conspiracy" (*weltbürgerliche Verschwörung des Kapitals*).[2]

In short, the title of Derrida's pamphlet reverses, and not without a certain sweet violence, the devaluation of cosmopolitanism that is already widely under way in the work of Marx. Because its value is apparently devalued according to an inexorable process that, from the celestial heights it reached in Kant's work, led the word into the hell of the "cosmopolitan Jew" (as *Weltjude* was translated) mentioned in *Mein Kampf* or the "rootless cosmopolitan" (*bezrodnie kosmopoliti*) targeted by Stalin's anti-Semitic campaigns starting in 1948.

Of course, Derrida knows all this all too well; elsewhere, he recalls the "ideological connotations with which modern anti-Semitism saddled the great tradition of a cosmopolitanism passed down from Stoicism or Pauline Christianity to the Enlightenment and to Kant."[3] What Derrida states less explicitly, though he is of course not ignorant of it either, is that cosmopolitanism, after its Kantian moment, also becomes synonymous with powerlessness or indifference, with political disengagement. This is something we can hear in the writings of the Italian patriot Giuseppe Mazzini, for example, when he opposes nationalism with cosmopolitanism in the following terms:

> I have heard many honorable men, animated by the best intentions, declare this standard of *Nationality* that we cherish to be dangerous and retrograde. They told me: "We are more advanced than you," and they continued: "We no longer believe in the nation, we believe in humanity: we are *Cosmopolitans*." . . . We are all Cosmopolitans, if by Cosmopolitanism we understand the love and brotherhood of all, and the destruction of all barriers that separate the Peoples and provide them with opposite interests. But can that be all? . . . Our work aims at transforming ideas into reality; we have to *organize*, if I may say so, not thought, but *action*. Now every organization that is to concretely affect reality requires a starting point and a goal. . . . For us, the end is humanity; the pivot, or point of support is man, the isolated *individual*. Therein lies almost all the difference between us and the Cosmopolitans, but it is a major difference.[4]

The cosmopolitan, Mazzini says in sum, jumps all alone beyond the nation, directly to the scale of humanity. And this is why he cannot give himself the means to intervene concretely; he does not act and is only able to speak in isolation and in the name of great principles, whereas the Mazzinian nationalist on the contrary seeks out the point of support for alliances *between nations*, as can be seen in his 1863 call to Serbian and Hungarian patriots to fight together against Austrian oppression. What

Mazzini's nationalism places up against cosmopolitanism is thus ultimately what Marcel Mauss called an *inter-nation*.[5]

So true is this that there will also be convinced internationalists who will, almost everywhere, turn their backs on cosmopolitanism in a gesture whose logic was, at bottom, already sketched out in section 209 of Hegel's *Elements of the Philosophy of Right*. There, one could read that, on the one hand, "A *human being counts as such because he is a human being*, not because he is a Jew, Catholic, Protestant, German, Italian, etc." And on the other, a warning that reminds us that "this consciousness" of humanity in each human, while of "infinite importance," can nonetheless also be frozen "in opposition to the concrete life of the state—for example, as *cosmopolitanism*."[6]

What good does it do to recall all these discourses, some very well known and others less so? Why mention them here? Simply to provide the measure for Derrida's singular gesture when he prints the mark of this title: "Cosmopolitans of All Lands, Yet Another Effort!"

If he no doubt does not hold a monopoly on the word in contemporary philosophy, to my knowledge, Derrida is the only person to have made cosmopolitanism into such an imperative and direct watchword through the interpellation of his exclamation point: "Cosmopolitans of All Lands, Yet Another Effort!" is an injunction for which, even in Derrida's work, one could find very few equivalents.

)) ((

"The Cosmopolitan," continues Mazzini a few lines after the ones I just cited, "stands alone at the center of an immense circle that extends itself around him, and whose limits are beyond his grasp" ("Nationality and Cosmopolitanism," 58). This image that once again attempts to state the cosmopolitan's political powerlessness, his or her lack of a point of support for action can, as long as we hear it differently, also gesture toward the horizon from whose perspective cosmopolitanism demands to be re-thought today. For the circle Mazzini speaks of is not without re-calling the figure of the globe in its global or globalized form, or else of what was once called the ecumene, in other words the in-habited space of the Earth's surface (the word comes from the Greek *oikein*: to inhabit, in the expression *oikoumenê gé*).

In a 1920 text called *The Nation*, Marcel Mauss was able to write: "Now that the ecumene forms a world, . . . there is no peo-ple that is not in direct or indirect relations with the others."[7] Yet faced with this confident affirmation of the unity of the inhabited earthly world, faced with this faith in the being-world and the being-one of this world that is ours, Mazzini's image insists and interrogates: "Alone at the center of an immense circle . . . whose limits are beyond his grasp," the cosmopolitan may indeed have something to do precisely with the inaccessible, with the infi-nitely other that, under every step in this world, digs out the abyss of what we indeed must call an *unworld*.

But let's not go too quickly.

It is slowly, patiently, and with precaution that we must let the other figure of cosmopolitanism come—the one that has not yet arrived or that we have perhaps not yet perceived.

As an attempt to grope closer to it, one can already try to return to Kant, as Derrida did in such a striking way, after two centuries of constant devaluation of cosmopolitan discourse. It would then be a matter of rereading Kant's cosmopolitical writ-ings, of soliciting them once again, as Derrida had begun to do by interrogating the limitations that, in *Perpetual Peace*, oversee the Kantian idea of a hospitality that is nonetheless qualified as universal.[8] But, in order to begin to listen for a cosmopolitanism to come, we must no doubt reopen its stakes to even vaster ex-panses without restricting it, as a certain reception of Derrida has done, to the theme of hospitality.[9]

This is why, in the preceding pages, I attempted to lend an atten-tive ear to what might be announced in another site of the Kantian cosmopolitical corpus, namely the end of the *Anthropology*. There,

Kant is about to characterize the human race as a "multitude of persons" who are "destined by nature to develop . . . into a *cosmopolitan society* (*cosmopolitismus*)."[10] Yet before getting to this cosmopolitical characterization of humanity, and speaking of the human being as a *"terrestrial* rational being," Kant writes (as we read earlier):

> We shall not be able to name its character because we have no knowledge of the *non-terrestrial* beings that would enable us to indicate their characteristic property and so to characterize this terrestrial being among rational beings in general. It seems, therefore, that the problem of indicating the character of the human species is absolutely insoluble, because the solution would have to be made through experience by means of the comparison of two species of rational being, but experience does not offer us this possibility. (*Anthropology*, 225)

Here, I am once again insisting, there is a gesture with a triple consequence: (1) Humanity is structurally *projected toward an extra-earthly space* from which it is called to be characterized; but (2) it can define itself there only by undefining itself in a movement of *comparison without a comparative term*; and (3) this movement is *horizontal* rather than vertical, in the sense that it seems a priori to imply none of the hierarchies that traditionally situate the human as a mortal and a rational animal, between the beast and the god, above the one and below the other.

In the triple reach of this gripping gesture of the last pages of the Kantian *Anthropology*, a possible figure for another cosmopolitanism might be sketched out. It *might* be, I say in the conditional, for what seems thus to be announced as this triple opening cracks ajar closes right back up again, already in the next paragraph: (1) We immediately return (226) to the ground of the terrestrial ecumene so that the human being can be differentiated "among the living inhabitants of this earth"; (2) the human is then very classically characterized in comparison with the animal (the human is a *rational animal*, says Kant); and (3) the human being is thus understood as being raised *above* animality following a *vertical* ascension for which the almost comical question of his standing posture is in a way the metaphor ("is the human being originally destined to walk on four feet . . . or on two feet?" asks Kant, and one can imagine the answer).

These contrary or contradictory movements provide the background against which, at the end of the *Anthropology*, the cosmopolitical question emerges as Kant takes it up from the Stoics and sends it our way. But why insist, as I have done, on the reach of this comparative indefinition of humanity? Why is it important to recall that in the Kantian text it provides a *precondition* for the formulation of cosmopolitical stakes, a kind of premise to which we can then return as a way to give ourselves the chance to reinvent or rethink an idea whose devaluation threatens it with liquidation?

It is because at stake is no more and no less than the concept of the world, of this *kosmos* of which cosmopolitanism should perhaps be above all the questioning auscultation, even before being a determined way of inhabiting, exploiting, or sharing it.

)) ((

Over the course of the long history of cosmopolitanism, starting with its Stoic sources through today and perhaps into tomorrow, the proposition of a world inhabited in common by all members of the human species has always been very closely accompanied and even explicitly sustained by the thetic and stubborn affirmation of the distinction between animality and humanity, as if it were a question of reassuring ourselves of the impermeability of the border separating them. In just a moment, we'll be reading this in Cicero and Augustine: The comparative gesture that defines the animal and the human in relation to one another—this hierarchizing movement that Kant's *Anthropology*, as we saw, seems for an instant to want to topple over into horizontality—this gesture may well be constitutive of every cosmopolitical horizon. As we will verify, it may well provide its necessary premise.

Now this border between humanity and animality is one whose cracks and fissures Derrida constantly probed. He constantly explored its porosities[11] so as to make his meditation on the animal a privileged mode of access to the question of the world as such. The task that thus befalls us in order to bring about or allow for an other cosmopolitanism to come is perhaps to open up the concept and expose it (given that it shelters the word *kosmos* within it) to this deconstructing questioning bearing on the worldliness of the world as it is constituted *on the basis of* the comparison between the human and the animal. I will be getting to this in just a moment, but it is important beforehand to probe the constancy and recurrence of the comparative gesture starting with the most ancient cosmopolitical tradition.

As we know, the cynic Diogenes of Sinope is traditionally attributed with the paternity of the word *kosmopolitês*, which then becomes a major signifier all the way through late Stoicism.[12] Yet the Stoic concept of the citizen of the world, especially as it is outlined in Cicero's writing, appears as explicitly carried by and propped up on a comparative definition of humanity. This definition seems to serve to support cosmopolitical horizontality on the most solid of vertical hierarchies between human being and animal, as can be seen in a page from *De finibus bonorum et malorum* (3.64–67):

> The Stoics hold that the universe is ruled by divine will, and that it is virtually a single city and state shared by humans and gods [*quasi communem urbem et civitatem hominum et deorum*]. Each one of us is a part of this universe [*mundi esse partem*]. It follows naturally from this that we value the common good more than our own [*communem utilitatem nostrae anteponamus*]. . . . We use the parts of our body before we have learned the actual reasons why we have them. In the same way it is by nature that we have gathered together and

formed ourselves into civil societies [*ad civilem communitatem coniuncti et consociati sumus*]. . . . But though they hold that there is a code of law which binds humans together, the Stoics do not consider that any such code exists between humans and other animals. Chrysippus made the famous remark that all other things were created for the sake of humans and gods, but that humans and gods were created for the sake of their own community and society [*cetera nata esse hominum causa et deorum, eos autem communitatis et societatis suae*]; and so humans use animals for their own benefit with impunity. He added that human nature is such that a kind of civil code mediates the individual and the human race [*ut ei cum genere humano quasi civile ius intercederet*]: whoever abides by this code will be just, whoever breaches it unjust.[13]

One can see it: It is by constructing itself on the basis of the vertical comparison with animality that the cosmopolitical horizon opens up and its horizontal contract is constituted. And this is also the case if we turn to the other major source of modern cosmopolitanism, to the other tributary feeding its discourse, in Kant and beyond him, namely to its Christian moment as it is epitomized in an exemplary way in Saint Augustine's *Civitas Dei*. Here again, it is on the basis of the clearly affirmed dominance over the animal realm that the earthly *cosmopolis* is constructed. In effect, it's a citation from Genesis (1:26: "Let them [humans] have dominion over the fish of the sea, and over the fowl of the air, and over the cattle") that first inspires the following commentary: "He did not intend that His rational creature, made in His own image, should have lordship over any but irrational creatures: not man over man, but man over the beasts."[14] This statement in turn prepares and undergirds the formulation of the idea of Christian cosmopolitics in these terms (19.17):

For as long as this Heavenly City is a pilgrim on earth, she summons citizens of all nations [*ex omnibus gentibus cives evocat*], and in all languages brings together a society of pilgrims [*in omnibus linguis peregrinam colligit societatem*] in which no attention is paid to any differences in the customs, laws, and institutions by which earthly peace is achieved or maintained. She does not rescind or destroy these things, however. For whatever differences there are among the various nations, these all tend towards the same end of earthly peace [*terrenae pacis*].[15]

Why then thus underline this architectonic solidarity—that might in many ways seem trivial—between, on the one hand, the affirmation of the border separating humanity from animality and, on the other hand, the opening of the cosmopolitical horizon? Quite simply to take the measure, once again, of what happens to cosmopolitanism with Derrida. For even as he revives this rallying cry in an unheard-of manner for a future we no longer foresaw for it, he nonetheless seems radically to undermine its strongest and most ancient supports.

)) ((

What vacillates and trembles in Derrida is not only, as we know, the purity of the distinction between human being and animal (and even the very resource for the comparative gesture that distinguishes between them). But it is also and at the same time, according to a consequence whose necessity we now better understand, the possibility of a common world. Here is what can be read, in a particularly gripping formulation, at the beginning of the second volume of *The Beast and the Sovereign*:

> Neither animals of different species, nor humans of different cultures, nor any animal or human individual inhabit the same world as another, however close and similar these living individuals may be (be they humans or animals), and the difference between one world and another will remain always unbridgeable,

because the community of the world is always constructed, si-mulated by a set of stabilizing apparatuses, more or less stable, then, and never neutral, language in the broad sense, codes of traces being designed, among all living beings, to construct a unity of the world that is always deconstructible, nowhere and never given in nature. Between my world . . . what I call "my world"—and there is no other for me, as any other world is part of it—between my world and any other world there is first the space and the time of an infinite difference, an interruption that is incommensurable with all attempts to make a passage, a bridge, an isthmus, all attempts at communication, translation, trope, and transfer that the desire for a world or the want of a world, the being wanted a world will try to pose, impose, pro-pose, stabilize. There is no world, there are only islands.[16]

As striking as it may be, this formulation nonetheless does not give the full measure of what is at stake. For it is not only the nat-uralness of the common world that Derrida is contesting (a nat-uralness that, from the Stoics to Kant and perhaps beyond, founds the cosmopolitical project as the destiny of humanity). It is also and above all, as we can hear in "Rams," the world's preex-istence, its antecedence over the address from an I to a you: "As soon as I speak to you and am responsible for you, or before you, there can no longer, essentially, be any world. No world can any longer support us, serve as mediation, as ground, as earth, as foundation or as alibi. Perhaps there is no longer anything but the abyssal altitude of a sky."[17]

In other words, before you and me, there is nothing, nothing that precedes us, nothing between us that allows us to say "we." This is what, taking up Hegel's quip about Spinoza, we might describe as the fundamentally *acosmic* nature of address or response in Derrida—on the condition that we immediately spec-ify that the aforementioned acosmism is in no way opposed to cosmopolitanism, but rather its condition of possibility yet to come.[18]

However unheard of it may be, however unthinkable and unthought, this idea of cosmopolitanism would share at least one characteristic with the habitual sense of the word that Mazzini was able to presuppose in his critique: the absence of mediation. "The Cosmopolitan," wrote Mazzini, "stands alone at the center of an immense circle that extends itself around him, and whose limits are beyond his grasp." All alone is what the I from the poem by Celan also is, the poem of which "Rams" is the patient and minute meditation. Still commenting on its last line (*die Welt ist fort, ich muss dich tragen*), Derrida in effect continues:

> Perhaps there is no longer anything but the abyssal altitude of a sky. I am alone in the world right where there is no longer any world. Or again: I am alone in the world as soon as I owe myself to you, as soon as you depend on me, as soon as I bear, and must assume, head to head or face to face, without third, mediator, or go-between, without earthly or worldly ground, the responsibility for which I must respond in front of you for you. ("Rams," 158)

One should thus say in all rigorousness that it is the I-you—the I to you or the you to me—that, without mediation, in the epochal suspension of the world, finds itself immediately projected to a *planetary* scale. On the condition of understanding this word, as Derrida does, from the perspective of its ancient history, of what still resonates within it of an old, immemorial errancy.

> The Greek noun leaves its trace there. Errancy is bound to be planetary. *Planêtes* means "wandering," "nomadic," and it is sometimes said of errant animals. . . . *Planêtikos* means unstable, turbulent, agitated, unpredictable, irregular; *planos* is used to describe an errant course but also a digression, for example, in the articulation of a discourse, of a written text. (Derrida, "Rams," 153)

Derrida mentions this planetary or planetic destinerrancy in the context of a reading of Celan over the course of which he refers several times to the Heideggerian meditation on the concept of world. And this is why it is impossible not to hear an echo here of one of Heidegger's formulations describing the Earth under the grasp of modern technology, not only as the unworld of error or errancy (*Unwelt der Irrnis*), but also and most importantly as an erring orb or crazed star (*Irrstern*). As if our planet, from the point of view of the history of being (*seyngeschichtlich*), did not have or no longer had a determined place in the universe.[19] This formulation concludes a passage that, without taking recourse to the word *cosmopolitanism* (Heidegger hardly ever uses it), nonetheless mentions the major motifs that are generally associated with it.

> Just as the distinction between war and peace has become untenable, the distinction between "national" and "international" has also collapsed. Whoever thinks in "a European way" today, no longer allows himself to be exposed to the reproach of being an "internationalist." But he is also no longer a nationalist, since he thinks no less about the well-being of the other nations than about his own.[20]

It is thus as if, for better or for worse, cosmopolitanism was also in solidarity with the unfurling of technology that transforms the world into an unworld (*Unwelt*). In other words into an acosmic space like the one where the *Sputnik* traveled, that first artificial satellite that Heidegger, in his series of three lectures called *On the Way to Language*,[21] mentions several times. In effect, this flying object thrown out into the cosmos emerges four times in Heidegger's lectures, thus provoking an interruption, something one would almost like to call a stunning and sidereal [*sidérale et sidérante*] collision with his meditation on a poem by Stefan George: "Countless people look upon this 'thing' *Sputnik* . . . as a wonder, this 'thing' that races around in a worldless 'world'-space [*das in einem weltlosen "Welt"-Raum umherrast*]" (62).

The repeated quotation marks—sorts of intermittent beeps like those the first *Sputnik* emitted—signal that the concepts of thing and world have, to Heidegger's eyes, been emptied of their meaning, that they, too, are traveling in the void. In this void on the basis of which the division of our world is nonetheless organized, for Heidegger further writes on, as if he were imagining the screenplay for a science fiction episode: "The battle for the dominion of the earth has entered its decisive phase. The all-out challenge to secure dominion over the earth [*die vollständige Herausforderung der Erde in die Sicherung der Herrschaft über sie*] can be met only by occupying an ultimate position beyond the earth from which to establish control over the earth" (*On the Way to Language*, 105).

If we follow Heidegger, it is thus from the point of view of this acosmic unworld that is the cosmos, it's from the point of view of the battle raging there, from the point of view of this cosmic politics or this cosmopolitics of a new type that *access* to our world is being configured and distributed. Starting with the sensible, perceptual access to it, in other words, what we can see or hear of it right here, down here, since we look increasingly with satellite eyes, just as we listen with ears in orbit. One could speak here, as I have suggested, of a "geopolitics of the sensible." Or else of *cosmetopolitics*, allowing yet another significance of the word *kosmos* to resonate, namely cosmetics as a touch-up of the sensible.

But what Derrida's acosmic cosmopolitanism demands that we think is that the unworld of planetary or planetizing destinerrancy is not only the Archimedean point from the perspective of which dominion over the earth is established. It is not only there where, for Heidegger, modern technology has caused the desert and power to increase. It is also, *in an indissociable way*, there where the other, with every step and at every instant, reserves and holds itself [*se reserve, se tient*] as utterly other.

)) ((

No one, no philosopher, after Kant, has seriously imagined other faraway worlds populated by inhabitants that would be so many nonearthly reasonable beings, unknowable comparatives for humanity. But, although not supposing it *inhabited*, there is at least one thinker who, unlike Heidegger, and as an answer explicitly addressed to him, considered that the cosmos, the cosmos of modern technoscience, was partly *inhabitable*. A little bit inhabitable, for a lapse of time perhaps destined to grow in length.

In a short text called "Heidegger, Gagarin, and Us,"[22] written just after the first manned space flight, which, on April 12, 1961, carried the Soviet astronaut Yuri Gagarin into orbit, Emmanuel Levinas writes:

> Technology wrenches us out of the Heideggerian world and the superstitions surrounding *Place*. From this point on, an opportunity appears to us: to perceive men outside the situation in which they are placed, and let the human face shine in all its nudity. . . . What is admirable about Gagarin's feat is certainly not his magnificent performance at Luna Park which impresses the crowds; it is not the sporting achievement of having gone further than the others and broken the world records for height and speed. . . . What perhaps counts most of all is that he left the Place. For one hour, man existed beyond any horizon—everything around him was sky.[23]

One might think one hears some distant echo of Mazzini while reading the description of this man, who, "alone at the center of an immense circle . . . whose limits are beyond his grasp," is surrounded by nothing but sky. This man whose territory has become ultraplanetary and who thus seems to incarnate in an exemplary way the figure of an acosmism for which, as Derrida writes in "Rams," "perhaps there is no longer anything but the abyssal altitude of a sky."

It is, however, in an entirely different way that Derrida, for his part, calls up the image of the cosmonaut in a peculiar sequence in *Circumfession*: "I have neither up nor down, like the squirrel climbing up and down horizontally, the form of my world, a literature that is apparently, like the very look of my writing, cosmonautical, floating in weightlessness."[24] Here, the cosmonautical is slanted to the animal side; it, too, is bent toward animality. Or at least it cannot be reduced to the "human face in all its nudity" as Levinas describes it, for it is as if, with Derrida, the comparative indefinition of humanity that we saw peep through at the end of Kant's *Anthropology* were becoming general and structural, constitutive of an acosmic I-you from the perspective of which is announced a cosmopolitanism to come.[25]

Of this other idea of cosmopolitanism—which has no doubt not yet arrived or that we have perhaps not yet recognized—the possibility would be inscribed neither in a human nature nor in a destiny of humanity, nor in the stable and reassuring concept of some *zoon politikon* or *animal rationale*. To the contrary, it is barely cracked open each time that, in an I-to-you or a you-to-me, in an addressed gaze or listening (are there any that are not addressed?), the world, like humanity, steals away and ends.

Notes

A Little Bit of Tourism . . .

1. This is what Geoffrey Bennington forcefully recalls in his fine book *Frontières kantiennes* (Paris: Galilée, 2000), 16. "There will be peace (which must be perpetual in order to be peace) only in an international dynamic. . . . In order to be perpetual, peace must perpetually defer its perpetuity. Peace can thus not *be declared* but at most *be announced* as perpetually to come, in the guise of a promise promised forever and thus never kept" (TN: translation mine). My readings of Kant owe much to Bennington's remarkable analyses, which also devote a few pages to Kant's mentions of extraterrestrials (61–62).

2. See Carl Schmitt, *The Concept of the Political*, trans. George Schwab (Chicago: University of Chicago Press, 1995), 54.

3. We who have become *intercosmonauts* since, though we cannot afford a trip to the moon, we can already explore the planet Mars with software such as Google Earth.

4. The idea of *terraforming* or *ecogenesis* has inspired a vast literature, not only in science fiction but also in scientific journals such as *Science* (where Carl Sagan published a 1960 article, "The Planet Venus," that considered how planting algae might lead to a reduction of the greenhouse effect in Venus's atmosphere).

5. An entirely relative and perhaps legendary panic, as Pierre Lagrange suggests. See "La guerre des mondes n'a pas eu lieu," in the special edition of the *Monde diplomatique* (no. 664, July 2009) titled "Extraterrestrials between Science and Popular Culture."

6. Steven J. Dick traces out this tradition in *The Plurality of Worlds: The Extraterrestrial Life Debate from Democritus to Kant* (Cambridge: Cambridge University Press, 1984). Michael J. Crowe takes up the history of philosophical aliens where Dick ends his (see *The Extraterrestrial Life Debate, 1750–1900* [New York: Dover, 1999]), but one is forced to recognize that after Kant, the debate seems to have moved from philosophy to the history of science, with the exception of several brief remarks and parerga by Schopenhauer or Feuerbach. From Feuerbach, we will extract the following lines from *The Essence of Christianity*: "There may certainly be thinking beings besides men on the other planets of our solar system [*denkende Wesen auf den übrigen Planeten unseres Sonnensystems*]. But by the supposition of such beings we do not change our standing point [*verändern wir nicht unsern Standpunkt*]. . . . In fact, we people [*beleben*] the other planets, not that we may place there different beings from ourselves, but *more* beings of our own or of a similar nature [*mehr solche oder ähnliche Wesen, wie wir*]." *The Essence of Christianity*, introduction by Wolfgang Vondey (New York: Barnes and Noble, 2004), 13–14. With Kant, we will be arguing exactly the opposite case.

7. This is what the previously cited historical works of Steven J. Dick and Michael J. Crowe do not take into account. To my knowledge, the only people to have taken the pages Kant devotes to inhabitants of other worlds seriously *philosophically* are David L. Clark, in a remarkable article called "Kant's Aliens: The *Anthropology* and Its Others (*Centennial Review* 2 [Fall 2001]: 201–89); and Antoine Hatzenberger ("Kant, les extraterrestres et nous," in *Kant, les Lumières et nous,* ed. Abdelaziz Labib and Jean Ferrari [Tunis: Maison arabe du livre, 2008]). I thank my friend Elie During for pointing out this second study. It overlaps in many aspects with the hypotheses I sketched out at the invitation of Cyril Neyrat for a brief essay that was already called "Kant chez les extraterrestres. La philosofiction du sujet assiégé" (*Vertigo*, no. 32 [2007]).

8. See Carl Schmitt, *Theory of the Partisan*, trans. G. L. Ulmen (1963; New York: Telos, 2007), 80 (Schmitt speaks of *Kosmopiraten* and of *Kosmopartisanen*). See also "El orden del mundo después de la segunda guerra mundial," *Revista de Estudios Politicos*, no. 122 (1962):19–36, on the "appropriation of cosmic space." These are

questions we will have to patiently revisit using *The Nomos of the Earth*, trans. G. L. Ulmen (1950; New York: Telos, 2003).

9. Hannah Arendt, in *Lectures on Kant's Political Philosophy* (Chicago: University of Chicago Press, 1992), is no doubt the first to have shown that if Kant never wrote a "Fourth Critique," if his late writing cannot be gathered into a veritable "political philosophy," this is because this political philosophy is contained in a latent form in the *Critique of the Power of Judgment*, and in particular in his "aesthetics" (see Arendt, *Lectures,* in particular 61–65). In his *Politics of Friendship* (trans. George Collins [London: Verso, 2006], 130–31), Jacques Derrida speaks of Carl Schmitt and of a "hyper-politicization" that would be like the "chiasmus of a double hyperbole." "The less politics there is, the more there is." Following this alogical or paradoxical logic, if Kant and Schmitt, as we will see, are the theoreticians of a certain *end* of the political, then they are also, and each one for radically different reasons, theoreticians of a *hyperpolitics* that even politicizes aesthetics. The *distribution of the sensible* Jacques Rancière discusses (and to which we will return) follows this line of thinking, without, however, clarifying its geopolitical stakes.

1. Star Wars

1. Ronald Reagan Presidential Library, http://www.reagan.utexas.edu/archives/speeches/1987/092187b.htm.

2. This is the argument made, for example, by the writer Norman Spinrad in a strange article ("Quand "la guerre des étoiles" devient réalité") published by *Le Monde diplomatique* (July 1999). He argues: "Jerry Pournelle . . . , a science fiction writer and former president of the Science Fiction Writers of America . . . met Richard Allen who would become a national security adviser in President Ronald Reagan's new administration. . . . In November 1980, Jerry Pournelle set a Citizens' Advisory Council on National Space Policy into place. This organization resembled a lobby founded by private individuals whose goal was to influence the new Republican administration toward the creation of a visionary program of human spaceflight. . . . His avowed strategy consisted in getting the Reagan administration to accept the idea that it was possible to construct a

technological shield that would destroy enemy missiles in flight and would thus make the United States invulnerable to nuclear attack" (translation mine). One should nonetheless emphasize the fact that this collusion between military strategy and science fiction is not new, as Columba Peoples's study ("Haunted Dreams") shows in the remarkable series of texts gathered by Natalie Bormann and Michael Sheehan, *Securing Outer Space* (London: Routledge, 2009). Recalling the beginnings of the conquest of space in Germany from the 1920s to the 1940s with the foundation of an association for journeys into space (VfR for Verein für Raumschiffahrt, 1927), then with the development of the V-1 and V-2 missiles, Peoples writes: "Operating as something of an amateur society, testing prototypes somewhat haphazardly . . . the VfR's ambitious visions for space were frequently limited by a lack of funds and resources. An early opportunity to get some financing for the rocket experiments came with sponsorship from the promoters of Fritz Lang's 1929 science fiction film *Frau im Mond (Girl on the Moon)*, where the promoters hoped for a show of rocketry at the film's premiere. . . . It is likely that it was the publicity around the *Frau im Mond* premiere that alerted the efforts of the VfR to the German military" (93).

3. Al Gore, "Moving beyond Kyoto," *New York Times,* July 1, 2007. http://www.nytimes.com/2007/07/01/opinion/01gore.html?page wanted=all.

4. Frank White is the person who popularized this expression in his book *The Overview Effect: Space Exploration and Human Evolution* (New York: Houghton Mifflin, 1987). Considering the possibility of interplanetary travel across greater and greater distances, the author, clearly subject to the lyrical enthusiasm of so many utopians, imagines a future where Earthlings expatriated into the solar system "will cease to identify with Earthbound nation-states," and even with "Earth itself": "Like those in the liberated colonies in North America, they will jealously guard their incipient independence. . . . Someday an astronaut, finding himself or herself on the edge of the solar system, will look back . . ." (133). This much is clear: Here, as in so many of the dominant discourses in the United States, extraterrestrial space is a new America *in potentia*.

5. Carl Schmitt, "The Legal World Revolution" (1978), trans. G. L. Ulmen, *Telos* 72 (Summer 1987): 88 (my emphasis; TN: translation

modified). Almost forty years later, this sentence echoes another one I've already cited from *The Concept of the Political,* trans. George Schwab (Chicago: University of Chicago Press, 1995): "Humanity as such cannot wage war because it has no enemy, at least not on this planet" (54).

6. The dangers presented by this kind of refuse have recently become an object of heightened international awareness after China launched an attempted antisatellite weapon on January 11, 2007: The destruction from the Earth of an old satellite produced almost a thousand detected objects (more than ten centimeters wide). The risks are many, and they are exponential: Besides the possible fall-out on earth (which up until now has been limited to several attested cases), there is a fear of a multiplication of collisions with machines, whether or not they are inhabited, launched into space or into orbit. As William J. Broad explained in the *New York Times* ("Orbiting Junk, Once a Nuisance, Is Now a Threat," February 6, 2007): "For decades, space experts have worried that a speeding bit of orbital debris might one day smash a large spacecraft into hundreds of pieces and start a chain reaction, a slow cascade of collisions that would expand for centuries, spreading chaos through the heavens. . . . Now, experts say, China's test on Jan. 11 of an antisatellite rocket that shattered an old satellite into hundreds of large fragments means the chain reaction will most likely start sooner. If their predictions are right, the cascade could . . . eventually threaten to limit humanity's reach for the stars." In the feature-length animated film by the Pixar studios, *Wall-e* (2008), there is a shot that clearly alludes to this difficulty in leaving the earth.

7. A recent ad campaign launched in October 2009 by New Zealand's Office of Tourism praised the virgin spaces of this region of the planet with the slogan: "Welcome to New Zealand, the last new world."

8. The disaster movie by Roland Emmerich, *2012,* takes up this same motif but limits it symptomatically to earthly space: The arks don't take survivors anywhere else, to any kind of outside, but allow them simply to float at the surface of the floodwaters while they wait for better days. On a website placed under the responsibility of the fictive Institute for Human Continuity, the marketing campaign for the film ("viral" marketing, as we now say) offered the possibility of

signing up for the chance to win a seat on one of these arks. Many people seem to have signed up, and apparently in all seriousness.

9. I'll be citing the UN's resolutions and treaties as they were published on the site for the UNOOSA (United Nations Office for Outer Space) at www.unoosa.org.

10. This treaty, known as the Outer Space Treaty, was adopted on December 19, 1966, and went into effect on October 10, 1967.

11. This "Moon Agreement" was adopted on December 5, 1979, and went into effect on July 11, 1984, even though only a few countries had signed it (the major powers dominating the space race are notably absent from its signatories).

12. Bormann and Sheehan, *Securing Outer Space*. (I owe this reference to the generous vigilance of my friend Gil Anidjar.)

13. Full Spectrum Dominance is the key concept of Vision for 2020, a document published in 1997 by the U.S. Space Command, itself founded in 1985 before being transformed into the U.S. Strategic Command in 2002. Three years later, in a 2000 report called "Rebuilding America's Defenses," the neoconservative organization Project for the New American Century, a kind of think tank with incredible influence under the Bush administration, didn't hesitate to affirm the need to "control the new 'international commons' of space and 'cyber-space,'" as if the very idea of a *commons*, which in principle forbade any national sovereignty, were compatible with unilateral appropriation. In 2001, in its recommendations and warnings against the possibility of a "space Pearl Harbor," a commission presided over by the future defense secretary Donald Rumsfeld (Commission to Assess United States National Security Space Management and Organization) reiterated the necessity of an American militarization of cosmic space deemed compatible with the engagements of the United States according to the terms of the Outer Space Treaty: "There is no blanket prohibition in international law on placing or using weapons in space, applying force from space to earth or conducting military operations in and through space." All these texts are available on different websites. As I reread these pages, it seems that Barack Obama's politics concerning the occupation of the cosmos is being directed toward a radical downsizing.

14. Carl Schmitt, *Glossarium: Aufzeichnungen der Jahre 1947–1951* (Berlin: Duncker und Humblot, 1991) (TN: translation mine). I will not

enter here into the sad and uninteresting polemic that, even more than for Heidegger, tore through France concerning Schmitt. Must one read, comment, and teach Carl Schmitt? His engagement in the Nazi cause is undeniable and widely documented, starting in his own works. Yet however much it may trouble those who seek to reduce his work to this engagement as a way of reassuring themselves by relegating him to silence, his thinking goes much further than this, as Etienne Balibar in particular has shown in the fine and equitable preface to one of Schmitt's most controversial works. See *Le Léviathan dans la doctrine de l'Etat de Thomas Hobbes,* French translation by Denis Trierweiler (Paris: Le Seuil, 2002).

15. Carl Schmitt, *The Nomos of the Earth,* trans. G. L. Ulmen (1950; New York: Telos, 2003), 39.

16. Carl Schmitt, "El orden del mundo después de la segunda guerra mundial," *Revista de Estudios Politicos,* no. 122 (1962), 24 (TN: translation mine).

17. Schmitt, *Nomos of the Earth,* 67, translation modified. *Das griechische Wort für die erste Landnahme als erste Raum-Teilung und Einteilung, für die Ur-Teilung und Ur-Verteilung ist: Nomos.*

18. Carl Schmitt, "Appropriation/ Distribution/ Production: An Attempt to Determine from *Nomos* the Basic Questions of Every Social and Economic Order," which Schmitt himself presents as "a seventh corollary to *Nomos of the Earth.*" (TN: The English translation is printed as an appendix to *Nomos of the Earth,* 324–35.)

19. See Schmitt, *Nomos of the Earth,* 80, "Not every invasion or temporary occupation is a land appropriation that founds an order [*eine Ordnung begründende Landnahme*]. In world history [*Weltgeschichte*], there have been many acts of force [*Gewaltakte*] that have destroyed themselves quickly. Thus, every seizure of land [*Wegnahme des Landes*] is not a *nomos,* although conversely, *nomos,* understood in our sense of the term, always includes a land-based order and orientation [*eine bodenbezogene Ortung und Ordnung*]."

20. Carl Schmitt, *Land und Meer: Eine weltgeschichtliche Betrachtung* (1942; Stuttgart: Klett-Cotta, 2008), 7 (TN: translation mine).

21. Schmitt, *Nomos of the Earth,* 42 ("*keine sinnfällige Einheit von Raum und Recht, von Ordnung und Ortung*").

22. On the role of the maritime analogy in the constitution of a law of outer space, see Jill Stuart's remarks in "Unbundling Sovereignty, Territory, and the State in Outer Space," in *Securing Outer Space*, ed. Bormann and Sheehan, 11 and 21. Judge Helmut Tuerk, the vice president of the International Tribunal for the Law of the Sea, provided the reminder that the legal solution that consists in considering interplanetary space as *res communis humanitatis* ("common human heritage") gained sway based on the model adopted for the deep seabed that declares it beyond national jurisdiction" ("The Negotiation of the 'Moon Agreement,'" a paper delivered at the Space Law Symposium held in Vienna under the auspices of the UNOOSA on March 23, 2009, on the occasion of the thirtieth anniversary of the "Moon Agreement.") On the *nautics* of space (which can be found in cosmonauts and their spaceships), see Caterina Resta's comments in her beautiful essay on Schmitt (*Stato mondiale o nomos della terra: Carl Schmitt tra universo e pluriverso* [Milan: Antonio Pellicani Editore, 1999], 38): "The 'marine' lexicon persists in these new spaces: in the air and interstellar space as well as the ether and telecommunications," in other words, internauts who *navigate* on the internet (where the maritime figure of the pirate has also pursued a handsome posterity). This conjunction did not escape American neoconservatives from the Project for the New American Century, as you'll remember, see note 13.

23. Schmitt, *Nomos of the Earth,* 312.

24. "Land war in traditional European international law was *purely terrestrial;* sea war was *purely maritime*" (Schmitt, *Nomos*, 311).

25. "It is even a question of to what extent one can speak of a *horizon* of air war" (320). Yet the disappearance of this *horizontality* could already be detected, Schmitt says, "when large numbers of submarines came on the scene" (*Nomos*, 314).

26. Carl Schmitt, *Theory of the Partisan,* trans. G. L. Ulmen (New York: Telos, 2007), 21–22, 37, 76 (where the partisan is first compared to the "corsary of sea warfare" before being described as a representative of "a bit of true ground [*ein Stück echten Bodens*]."

27. As Geoffrey Bennington quite rightly puts it in his *Frontières kantiennes* when he speaks of the frontier in the sense of a "limit to civilization": "Beyond the frontier, the future is the past" (12; TN: translation mine). Yet the futurist inspiration—of Kubrick, for

example—also draws on the Nietzschean source of the eternal return, and even on Auguste Blanqui's. In his *Eternité par les astres*, Blanqui's hypothesis is that "the number of our doubles is infinite in both time and space" ([Paris: Librairie Germer Baillière, 1872], 74). Whatever the case may be, one could start with Maurice Blanchot's remarks ("Le bon usage de la science-fiction," *Nouvelle revue française*, no. 73 [January 1959], 91–100) as a way to think the strength of science fiction as a "remarkable expression of the prophetic function." As Blanchot further writes, "Prophets not only announce the future; they are the word of what cannot be and is nonetheless coming and what, through this coming, *makes the present impossible*" (94, my emphasis; TN: translation mine).

28. Schmitt, "El orden del mundo depués de la segunda guerra mundial," 25 (TN: translation mine).

29. As Schmitt himself wrote, as we saw, in "Appropriation/ Distribution/ Production," in *Nomos of the Earth,* 335.

30. Carl Schmitt, "Die legale Weltrevolution," *Der Staat* (Berlin, 1978), 3, 321–29 (TN: translation mine).

31. "*World-politics (Weltpolitik)* approaches its end and turns into *world-police (Weltpolizei),* which amounts to a dubious progress" ("Die legale," 3; TN: translation mine).

32. Schmitt, *Nomos of the Earth,* 86.

33. Schmitt says this over and over again, in all possible ways: "The appearance of vast free spaces and the land appropriation of a new world made possible a new European international law among states: an interstate structure. In the epoch of interstate international law, which lasted from the sixteenth to the end of the nineteenth century, there was real progress, namely a limiting and bracketing of European wars. This great accomplishment . . . arose solely from the emergence of a new spatial order—a balance of territorial states on the European continent in relation to the maritime British Empire and against the background of vast *free spaces*" (*Nomos*, 140, Schmitt's emphasis). And elsewhere: "The new interstate order of the European continent . . . had arisen *since the European land appropriation of the New World* (*Nomos,* 142, my emphasis). And finally: "This spatial order (*Raumordnung*) and its concept of balance (*Gleichgewichts-Vorstellung*) had as its *essential presupposition and foundation* the fact that the European Great

Powers had free spaces at their disposal for colonial expansion [*ein freier Raum kolonialer Expansion*] all over the Earth except in Europe, from the seventeenth to the nineteenth century" (*Nomos*, 161; TN: translation modified).

34. Schmitt, *Land und Meer*, 65–66 (translation mine).

35. Carl Schmitt, "Die geschichtliche Struktur des Gegensatzes von Ost und West," in *Staat, Grossraum, Nomos, Arbeiten aus den Jahren 1916–1969*, Berlin: Duncker und Humblot, 1955, 544 (TN: translation mine).

36. One of NASA's administrators, Michael D. Griffin, did not hesitate to declare in 2005 in the very serious *Washington Post* that "Humans Will Colonize the Solar System": "There will be more human beings who live off the Earth than on it. We may well have people living on the moon. We may have people living on the moons of Jupiter and other planets. We may have people making habitats on asteroids. We've got places that humans will go, not in our lifetime, but they will go there" (September 25, 2005).

37. Schmitt prefers this term to other designations, such as "hologeic" or "planetary."

38. Carl Schmitt, "Grossraum gegen Universalismus: Der völkerrechtliche Kampf um die Monroedoktrine," *Zeitschrift der Akademie für Deutsches Recht*, May 7, 1939, 333–37 (TN: translation mine).

39. Schmitt, *Nomos of the Earth*, 122. On Schmitt's critique of the "humanitarian" foundation of the League of Nations, see *Concept of the Political*, 54, "The concept of humanity is an especially useful ideological instrument of imperialist expansion, and in its ethical-humanitarian form it is a specific vehicle of economic imperialism." And again, "The genuine concept of humanity is expressed in [the League of Nations] only insofar as its actual activities reside in the humanitarian and not in the political field" (56). This is why, in a discussion of the practice of embargo, blockades, sanctions, or, in a word, of "international police," Schmitt can write, "The adversary is thus no longer called an enemy but a disturber of peace and is thereby designated to be an outlaw of humanity. A war waged to protect or expand economic power must, with the aid of propaganda, turn into a crusade and into the last war of humanity" (79). On the juridical history of the concept of humanity, see Daniel

Heller-Roazen, *The Enemy of All: Piracy and the Law of Nations* (New York: Zone, 2009), 147–62.

40. Schmitt, *Nomos of the Earth*, 296. On the genesis of the Schmittean expression *Weltbürgerkrieg* and on its posterity, see the excellent preface by Céline Jouin, "La guerre civile mondiale n'a pas eu lieu," in *La guerre civile mondiale: Essais 1943–1978* (Maisons-Alfort: editions ère, 2007), 7–27.

41. Schmitt, *Concept of the Political*, 54. As you will recall, the same sentence is repeated almost literally in Schmitt's last published text, "The Legal World Revolution": "Humanity as such and as a whole has no enemies on this planet" (88).

42. In France, the so-called Cometa report, written by a group that brought together officers and engineers from the French army and submitted to Jacques Chirac and Lionel Jospin in 1999, goes in this direction; in his preface, the general of the air force, Denis Letty, writes: "UFOs are now a part of our media environment; movies, television shows, books, ads, etc. that portray UFOs amply show this. Even though no identified threat has today been perceived in France, it seemed necessary to former students of the Institut des Hautes Etudes de Défense nationale (IHEDN) to evaluate the situation in this matter" (TN: translation mine). See *Les OVNIS et la Défense—Le rapport COMETA* (Paris: J'ai lu, 2006).

43. See Schmitt, *Concept of the Political*, 26: "The specific political distinction [*die spezifisch politische Unterscheidung*] to which political actions and motives can be reduced is that between friend and enemy [*ist die Unterscheidung von Freund und Feind*]. This provides a definition [*Begriffsbestimmung*, in other words a conceptual determination] in the sense of a criterion. . . . Insofar as it is not derived from other criteria, the antithesis of friend and enemy corresponds, in the political order [*für das Politische*] to the relatively independent criteria of other antitheses: good and evil in the moral sphere, beautiful and ugly in the aesthetic sphere, and so on. In any event it is independent. . . . The political enemy need not be morally evil or aesthetically ugly; he need not appear as an economic competitor, and it may even be advantageous to engage with him in business transactions. . . . The morally evil, aesthetically ugly, or economically damaging need not necessarily be the enemy; the morally good, aesthetically beautiful, and economically profitable

need not necessarily become the friend in the specifically political sense of the word. Thereby the inherently objective nature and autonomy of the political becomes evident by virtue of its being able to treat, distinguish, and comprehend the friend-enemy antithesis independently of other antitheses [*die seinsmässige Sachlichkeit und Selbständigkeit des Politischen zeigt sich schon in dieser Möglichkeit, einen derartig spezifischen Gegensatz wie Freund-Feind von anderen Unterscheidungen zu trennen und als etwas Selbständiges zu begreifen*]. In *Politics of Friendship*, trans. George Collins (London: Verso, 2005), Jacques Derrida qualifies Schmitt as "the last great metaphysician of politics" (247) because of his attachment to oppositional purity and the credit he accords to "oppositionality itself, ontological adversity" (249). Is this not in effect what brings Schmitt to say not only that politics as such depends on the opposition friend versus enemy, but also and above all, in the perspective that interests us here, that any order presupposes its clearly delimited outside? And if this "oppositionality" is in crisis, it is not only such and such a *nomos* that is dissolved; it's rather the notion itself of *nomos* that finds itself radically destabilized. If, in addition, it is true, as I have suggested, that Schmittean discourse, in the trajectory that leads it from land appropriations to the conquest of aerial and then cosmic space, continuously clings to a telluric anchoring attached to the value of presence, then the question Derrida poses touches on the very heart of the concept of politics: "What does 'politically' 'present' mean?" (132).

44. "*Der Krieg spielt sich dann in der Form des jeweils 'endgültig letzten Krieges der Menschheit' ab . . . über das Politische hinausgehend*" (Schmitt, *Theory of the Partisan*, 33). The last section of the *Theory of the Partisan* is called "From the Real Enemy to the Absolute Enemy" (*Vom wirklichen zum absoluten Feind*).

45. We will recall here the pages that Michel Foucault devoted to "indefinite medicalization" in 1974 ("Crise de la medicine ou crise de l'antimédecine?" in *Dits et ecrits*, II [Paris: Gallimard, 2001], 48). Whether or not one chooses to consider this boundless generalization of medical intervention within the horizon of a *biopolitics*, what is certain is that it is the symptom and sign for the fact that the conceptual purity of a Schmittean notion of politics has become impossible to locate.

46. I am citing the text of the *Code of Federal Regulations*, title 14, section 1211. One should note the definition's circularity.

47. And thus delivering a flagrant denial to ecumenical optimism and the cosmochristianism of certain activists of (geo)Christian faith. I recently came across an article in the Vatican newspaper (Francesco M. Valiante, "L'extraterrestre è mio fratello" [The extraterrestrial is my brother], *L'Osservatore romano*, March 14, 2008) in which the Jesuit Father José Gabriel Funes, with his Borgesian patronymic, declared: "To say it in Saint Francis's words, if we consider earthly creatures as 'brothers' and 'sisters,' why wouldn't we also speak of an 'extraterrestrial brother' [*di un "fratello extraterrestre"*]? He would still be a part of creation." The place of extraterrestrials in Christianity would deserve a full study of its own. Kant, in his *Theory of the Heavens* that we will be reading a bit later on, thus addresses the "question as to whether sin exercises its domination in other spheres of the solar system" (Immanuel Kant, *Universal Natural History and Theory of the Heavens*, trans. Olaf Reinhardt, in *Natural Science*, ed. Eric Watkins (Cambridge: Cambridge University Press, 2012), 306). Tommaso Campanella had already affirmed in his 1622 *Apologia pro Galileo*, that "if the inhabitants which may be in other stars are men, they did not originate from Adam and are not infected by his sin," so much so that they have no "need for redemption, unless they have committed some other sin" (cited in Michael J. Crowe, *The Extraterrestrial Life Debate, 1750–1900* [New York: Dover, 1999], 12–13).

48. The first sequence in *Men in Black*, a film we will be returning to, plays on this double meaning of the word *alien*. Among the Latin American immigrants trying to cross the southern border of the United States, one comes from much farther away than just Mexico: He comes from the cosmos.

49. The Roswell affair, the purported crash of an unidentified object near Roswell, New Mexico, in July 1947, is probably the most famous UFO story. Roland Emmerich's 1996 film *Independence Day* contains ample allusions to it.

50. As the French translators of *Nomos of the Earth* remark (*Le nomos de la terre*, trans. Lilyane Deroche-Gurcel, rev. Peter Haggenmacher [Paris: Presses universitaires de France, 2001], 328n14), "This citation does not appear in the place indicated" by Schmitt in Kant's

Doctrine of Right, "even if it does give the general idea." Kant writes: "Since the land [*Boden*] is the ultimate condition [*oberste Bedingung*] that alone makes it possible to have external things as one's own [*äussere Sachen als das Seine zu haben*], and the first right that can be acquired is possession and use of such things [*deren möglicher Besitz und Gebrauch das erste erwerbliche Recht ausmacht*], all such rights must be derived from the sovereign as *lord of the land*, or better, as the supreme proprietor of it [*von dem Souverän, als Landesherren, besser als Obereigenthümer*]." See Immanuel Kant, *The Metaphysics of Morals*, trans. Mary Gregor (Cambridge: Cambridge University Press, 1996), 99.

51. Kant, *Metaphysics of Morals*, II, §§12, 16.

52. Ibid., §16, 54: "*Alle Menschen sind ursprünglich in einem Gesamt-Besitz des Bodens der ganzen Erde.*" See also §13, 50–51: "The possession by all human beings on the earth which precedes any act of theirs that would establish rights (is constituted by nature itself) is an *original possession in common* [*ein ursprünglicher Gesamtbesitz*] (*communion possessionis originaria*), the concept of which is not empirical and dependent upon temporal conditions, like that of a supposed *primitive possession in common* [*eines uranfänglichen Gesamtbesitzes*] (*communion primaeva*), which can never be proved. Original possession in common is, rather, a practical rational concept [*ein praktischer Vernunftbegriff*]."

53. See Schmitt, *Nomos of the Earth*, 50 (TN: translation slightly modified): "For centuries, humanity had a mythical image of the earth, but no scientific understanding of it as a whole. There was no concept of the planet, of human compass and orientation [*Ortung*] common to all peoples. In this sense, there was no global consciousness and thus no political goal oriented to a common star. . . . In this context, we can disregard the philosophical generalizations of the Hellenistic period, which made a *cosmopolis* out of a *polis*, because they lacked a *topos*, and thus had no concrete order [*Ordnung*]." Glancing through the index of the two monumental volumes published by Günter Maschke that collect Schmitt's work from 1916 to 1978 (*Staat, Grossraum, Nomos*, and *Frieden oder Pazifismus? Arbeiten zum Völkerrecht und zur internationalen Politik, 1924–1978* (Berlin: Duncker und Humblot, 2005), one finds one single occurrence of the word "cosmopolitan," in the second volume:

"A status of citizen of the world (cosmopolitan) that would be immediate in terms of people's rights, has until now not been created, neither for all men nor for determined groups nor for isolated individuals [*Ein völkerrechtsunmittelbarer Status eines Weltbürgers (Kosmopoliten) ist bisher noch nicht geschaffen worden, weder für alle Menschen, noch für bestimmte Gruppen, noch für einzelne Individuen*]" (776; TN: translation mine). Günter Maschke comments on this statement in the following way: "One can read this as a variant on the fundamental Schmittean statement [*des Schmittischen Grundsatzes*] according to which 'humanity' is not a political concept [*kein politischer Begriff*] or as an allusion to Kant's "cosmopolitan right" [*Weltbürgerrecht*] (*ius cosmopoliticum*), which does not attain any legal dignity [*das keine juristische Dignität erreicht*] . . . and remains merely an ideological suggestion" (829n82). On the ties between Kantian cosmopolitism and the ancient Hellenistic tradition to which Schmitt briefly alludes in *Nomos of the Earth*, see Martha Nussbaum, "Kant and Stoic Cosmopolitanism," *Journal of Political Philosophy* 5, no. 1 (1997): 1–25.

54. Michel de Montaigne, *The Complete Essays* (1.26), trans. M. A. Screech (New York: Penguin, 1993), 176.

55. For a general view of Schmitt's use of this idea and of its sources, see Nestor Capdevila, "L'impérialisme entre inclusion exclusive et exclusion inclusive: Schmitt lecteur de Vitoria," in *Reconnaissance, identité et integration sociale*, ed. Christian Lazzeri and Soraya Nour (Paris: Presses Universitaires de Paris Ouest, 2009).

2. Kant in the Land of Extraterrestrials

1. Immanuel Kant, *Universal Natural History and Theory of the Heavens*, trans. Olaf Reinhardt, in *Natural Science*, ed. Eric Watkins (Cambridge: Cambridge University Press, 2012), 295.

2. Bernard Le Bovier de Fontenelle, *Conversations on the Plurality of Worlds*, trans. H. A. Hargreaves (Berkeley: University of California Press, 1990).

3. So great was the success of Fontenelle's *Conversations* that, at the time when Kant was writing his *Theory of the Heavens*, they had already been printed in eleven French editions and three German translations. See Steven J. Dick, *The Plurality of Worlds: The*

Extraterrestrial Life Debate from Democritus to Kant (Cambridge: Cambridge University Press, 1984).

4. Fontenelle, *Conversation on the Plurality of Worlds,* 44.

5. It remains to be known where this *philosofiction* should be situated in the complex cartography of the relations between philosophy and fiction about which Derrida did not hesitate to declare: "Not only could one show that all philosophical discourse presupposes a certain fictionality, but also that it takes regular recourse to some fiction. One would show that at a given moment, all philosophers have made fiction a keystone of their discourse: there is a moment when fiction, when the fictive example is a trial for the philosophical. It can be the dream in Descartes. In Husserl, there is a technique, a method of fictionality: fiction is the methodic instrument of phenomenology. It's theorized by Husserl [who] also says that the phenomenological analysis of the structures of consciousness can survive even the annihilation of the world in its totality. That means that every time I analyze the eidetic structures of phenomenological consciousness, I can suppose that the world does not exist. It's not a fiction among others: it's the fiction of the total annihilation of the world. And in a certain way, this fiction is presupposed as the very element of philosophical discourse" (Jacques Derrida, "Scènes des différences" [1996], interview with Mireille Calle-Gruber, *Littérature,* no. 142 [2006]: 27–28; TN: Translation mine.). We will return *in fine* to a certain Husserlian *philosofiction* when we read Husserl's surprising cosmic speculations in "Foundational Investigations of the Phenomenological Origin of the Spatiality of Nature: The Originary Ark, the Earth, Does Not Move" (which dates from May 1934, translated by Fred Kersten and revised by Leonard Lawlor in Maurice Merleau-Ponty, *Husserl at the Limits of Phenomenology,* ed. Leonard Lawlor with Bettina Bergo [Chicago: Northwestern University Press, 2001], 117–31).

6. Immanuel Kant, *Anthropology from a Pragmatic Point of View* (Cambridge: Cambridge University Press, 2006), 225.

7. Ibid., 236.

8. For example, in Kant's *Critique of Pure Reason,* "If it were possible to settle by any sort of experience whether there are inhabitants of at least some of the planets that we see, I might well bet everything I have on it. Hence I say that it is not merely an opinion but a

strong belief (on the correctness of which I would wager many advantages in life) that there are also inhabitants of other worlds" (Kant's *Critique of Pure Reason,* ed. and trans. Paul Guyer and Allen W. Wood [Cambridge: Cambridge University Press, 1999], 687), Besides these lines drawn from the third section of the *Critique of Pure Reason,* called "On Having Opinions, Knowing, and Believing," Kant also writes in the sixth section of "The Antinomy of Pure Reason" (in Kant, *Critique of Pure Reason,* 512) "that there could be inhabitants of the moon, even though no human being has ever perceived them, must of course be admitted, but this means only that in the possible progress of experience we could encounter them . . ." Later on, in his *Critique of the Power of Judgment,* Kant speaks more prudently of "opinion": "To assume rational inhabitants [*vernüftige Bewohner*] of other planets is a matter of opinion [*eine Sache der Meinung*]; for if we could approach more closely to other planets, which is intrinsically possible, we could determine by means of experience whether they exist or not; but we never will come close enough to other planets, so this remains a matter of opinion [*so bleibt es beim Meinen*]" (*Critique of the Power of Judgment,* ed. Paul Guyer, trans. Eric Matthews [Cambridge: Cambridge University Press, 2002], §91, 332).

9. As it stands, Kant concludes the cited passage with a Latin phrase (*vestigium hominis video,* "I see the trace of a human being") that gets rid of all doubt and draws the suspense to a close. This is, in fact, a slightly modified citation from an episode related in the preface to the third book of Vitruvius's *De architectura*: The Socratic philosopher Aristippus, having run ashore on the island of Rhodes, sees geometrical figures drawn in the sand and exclaims, "Let's keep hoping, I see traces of men" (*bene speremus, hominum enim vestigia video*). As for the "crop signs," this is something many researchers have investigated without being able to resolve the enigma. While writing these lines, I come across an article in the very serious *Courrier international* for *Directmatin* (no. 331, October 6, 2008, 16) where I read the following with something between disbelief and fascination: "Scientists are having an increasingly difficult time attributing this mysterious phenomenon (as a way of reassuring us) to a few tricksters cutting the wheat at night with a mower. . . . If one looks at these figures close-up, on site, several

elements remain unexplained: the wheat (or barley) stalks are not cut, but bent in a spiral form, as if they'd been crushed by a whirlwind. The stalks display very strange malformations; in the field, the air is often ionized. Finally, on the ground, iron microspheres have been found. No trace of footsteps can be found around these 'circles.' It would also be impossible to draw such complicated forms in the dark, all in one night. The most beautiful of the figures are born every summer in June and July in the most mysterious sites in England: Avebury, Slibury Hill, Stonehenge" (TN: translation mine).

10. "Most of the planets are certainly inhabited and those that are not will be at some stage," he nonetheless writes, thus leaving an open door to all possible cosmocolonizations (Kant, *Theory of the Heavens*, 297).

11. As Michael Crowe suggests (*The Extraterrestrial Life Debate, 1750–1900* [New York: Dover, 1999], 53), Kant seems to have forbidden the 1791 republication of the final chapters of his *Theory of the Heavens*, perhaps judging that "he had let his imagination roam too far."

12. "*Tout autre est tout autre*," translated by David Wills (in Jacques Derrida, *The Gift of Death* [Chicago: University of Chicago Press, 2007]) as "Every other (one) is every (bit) other": This sentence, whose first or second half (it depends) haunts the following pages, returns several times in Jacques Derrida's work. In "*Sauf le nom* (Post-Scriptum)," (trans. John Leavey Jr. in *On the Name*, ed. Thomas Dutoit [Stanford: Stanford University Press, 1995], one reads (emphasis mine): "The other is God or *no matter whom*, more precisely, no matter what singularity, as soon as any other is totally other" (74). If I will often insist on the *nondivine* character of Kantian extraterrestrials, who nonetheless harbor a radical alterity that differentiates them from a mere earthly *alter ego*, it will be as an attempt, beyond or in spite of the all too human projections we've just read (Newton, the Greenlander, the Hottentot, the ape . . .), to unearth not a vertical relation to the wholly other (human, between animal and god), but a horizontal one—a cosmopolitical one in the sense we will attempt to give this word dear to Kant: open as far as one can see onto the cosmos.

13. When actually one should take it very seriously, as Raphaël Lagier did in *Les Races humaines selon Kant* (Paris: Presses Universitaires de France, 2004). Gayatri Chakravorty Spivak (*Critique of*

Postcolonial Reason: Toward a History of the Vanishing Present
[Cambridge, Mass: Harvard University Press, 1999], 12–13) has also
shown how the Kantian sublime, which we will be discussing at
length later on, explicitly excludes *der rohe Mensch*, the "primitive"
(or "raw") human who is foreign to culture, "alien" to it.

14. Immanuel Kant, *On the Old Saw: That May Be Right in Theory But
It Won't Work in Practice*, trans. E. B. Ashton (Philadelphia: University of Pennsylvania Press, 1974), 42–43.

15. Immanuel Kant, *Conflict of the Faculties*, trans. Mary J. Gregor and
Robert Anchor, in *Religion and Rational Theology*, ed. Allen W.
Wood and George di Giovanni (Cambridge: Cambridge University
Press, 2001), 300 (§IV: "The Problem of Progress Is Not to Be Re-
solved Directly through Experience").

16. Kant, *Anthropology from a Pragmatic Point of View*, 4.

17. See in particular his letters to Marcus Herz on June 7, 1771, and February 21, 1772. In them Kant affirmed that he entertained "the hope
that by thus viewing my judgments impartially from the standpoint
of others some third view that will improve upon my previous
insight may be obtainable"; and he said that he wanted "to enlarge
its point of view from a microscopic to a general outlook that it
adopts in turn every conceivable standpoint, verifying the observations of each by means of all the others." These letters are cited by
Hannah Arendt in *Lectures on Kant's Political Philosophy* (Chicago:
University of Chicago Press, 1982), 42.

18. A note in the German edition established by Heiner Klemme (Immanuel Kant, *Kritik der Urteilskraft* [Hamburg: Felix Meiner Verlag,
2001], 435) specifies that Kant found the story of this Iroquois
sachem in François-Xavier de Charlevoix's work *Histoire et description générale de la Nouvelle-France, avec le Journal historique d'un
voyage fait par ordre du Roi dans l'Amérique Septentrionnale* (Paris,
1744). In one of the letters to the duchess of Lesdiguières that com-
pose the third volume (from August 1721, 322), one thus reads: "Iroquois going to Paris in 1666, to whom Royal Mansions were shown,
alongside all the other beauties of this great City, admired nothing
in them and would have preferred their Villages to the Capital of
the most resplendent Kingdom of Europe, if they hadn't seen the
rue de la Huchette where the Cook-Shops they always found

furnished with Meat of all kinds exerted a strong charm on them" (TN: translation mine).

19. A figure, as Simone Regazzoni has noted (*La filosfia di Lost* [Milan: Ponte alle Grazie, 2009], 29), Jacques Derrida had interrogated in his 2002–3 seminar dedicated to a combined reading of *Robinson Crusoe* and Heidegger (*The Beast and the Sovereign,* trans. Geoffrey Bennington [Chicago: University of Chicago Press, 2011]). Regazzoni notes that even as Derrida poses the question "What is an island?" he never actually answers it, limiting himself to saying, "There is no world, there are only islands." As if, as Regazzoni rightly comments, "as if a thinking of the island . . . inevitably brought us to rethink the world, to discuss the idea that there is a world, over there, out there: a unique, true and stable world we experience." Several pages later (35–36), following Deleuze's preface to *Difference and Repetition* ("a book of philosophy must be . . . a kind of science fiction"), Regazzoni considers what he names in his language a *fantafilosofia.* In other words, what I am calling here, after having sketched out a preliminary idea of it in the previously cited special number of the journal *Vertigo* (no. 32 [2007]: 6), a *philosofiction.*

20. Immanuel Kant, *Political Writings,* ed. H. S. Reiss, trans. H. B. Nisbet (Cambridge: Cambridge University Press, 1991), 238–39.

21. Of the power of judgment, Kant does indeed say that it "demonstrates autonomy" (*Critique of the Power of Judgment,* 27). But he immediately specifies that this autonomy is more precisely a *heautonomy* (from the Greek *heauton,* "oneself"): "Strictly speaking, one must call this . . . *heautonomy,* since the power of judgment does not give the law to nature nor to freedom, but solely to itself" (28). The autonomous or heautonomous insularity of the power of judgment within the critical enterprise (in relation to knowledge and reason) is what distinguishes Kant's aesthetics from Alexander Gottlieb Baumgarten's (*Aesthetica,* 1750). If Baumgarten can be considered the inventor of the word *aesthetica,* he continues to think of the philosophical territory of aesthetics as a kind of peninsula of knowledge: a weakened form of knowledge, given that it is sensory, less rigorous or reasoned than logical knowledge.

22. "The satisfaction *in the agreeable* is combined with interest" (Kant, *Critique of the Power of Judgment,* §3, 91). "The satisfaction *in the*

good is combined with interest. That is *good* which pleases by means of reason alone, through the mere concept. We call something *good for something* (the useful) that pleases only as a means; however, another thing is called *good in itself* that pleases for itself. Both always involved the concept of an end, hence the relation of reason to . . . willing, and consequently a satisfaction in the existence of an object or of an action, i.e. some sort of interest" (§4, 92–93).

23. In *Listen: A History of Our Ears* (trans. Charlotte Mandell [New York: Fordham University Press, 2008]), I tried to explore the consequences of this "structure of address" for musical listening.

24. In other contexts, Kant also speaks of *Hinsicht, Aussichtspunkt, Gesichtspunkt.* See, for example, in the Third Critique, §27 and §43. Schmitt, as you will recall, spoke of the *Standpunkt* of that earthly being (*Landwesen*) that is man. And this *Standpunkt*, which we translated as "standpoint," gave him his *Blickpunkt*, his "point of view." See above, Chapter 2, under the subhead "Appropriation and Distribution of Space."

25. Immanuel Kant, *Critique de la faculté de juger*, French translation published under the direction of Ferdinand Alquié, Folio Essais (Paris: Gallimard, 1985), 245.

26. This is the current consecrated scientific term to qualify research on forms of life in other worlds.

27. Kant, "Idea for a Universal History from a Cosmopolitan Perspective," in *Political Writings,* 41–53.

28. I discussed *effiction* in my *Membres fantômes* (Paris: Minuit, 2002), 21ff.

3. Cosmetics and Cosmopolitics

1. Friedrich Nietzsche, "From *Five Prefaces to Five Unwritten Books*," trans. Maximilian A. Mügge, in *Philosophical Writings*, ed. Reinhold Grimm and Caroline Molina y Vedia (New York: Continuum, 1997), 87.

2. First published in 1955, Jack Finney, *Invasion of the Body Snatchers* (New York: Simon and Schuster, 1998).

3. These fictive drones from 1999 look quite a bit like those the French police is considering using in suburbs declared "at risk." See Isabelle Mandraud, "Des drones pour suveiller banlieues et manifestations," *Le Monde*, October 12, 2007.

4. See Steven J. Dick, *The Plurality of Worlds: The Extraterrestrial Life Debate from Democritus to Kant* (Cambridge: Cambridge University Press, 1984), passim. Kant explicitly references Epicureanism over the course of his "Seventh Proposal" in his "Idea for a Universal History": "Should we . . . expect that the states, by an *Epicurean* concourse of efficient causes, should enter by random collisions (like those of small material particles) into all kinds of formations which are again destroyed by new collisions, until they arrive *by chance* at a formation which can survive in its existing form (a lucky accident which is hardly likely ever to occur); or should we assume as a second possibility that nature in this case follows a regular course in leading our species gradually upwards from the lower level of animality to the highest level of humanity. . . . Or should we rather accept the third possibility that nothing at all, or at least nothing rational, will anywhere emerge from all these actions and counter-actions among men as a whole, that things will remain as they have always been, and that it would thus be impossible to predict whether the discord which is so natural to our species is not preparing the way for a hell of evils to overtake us, however civilized our condition, in that nature by barbaric devastation, might perhaps again destroy this civilized state and all the cultural progress hitherto achieved?" (Immanuel Kant, *Political Writings*, ed. H. S. Reiss, trans. H. B. Nisbet (Cambridge: Cambridge University Press, 1991), 48, translation slightly modified). By referring to Epicurus's atomist doctrine, Kant is here playing—if one can actually speak of "playing" when confronted with these serious and anything but dated questions—with an ancient materialist tradition for which *there certainly exists* an infinite number of inhabited worlds. In the poetic exposé of Epicureanism that Lucretius gives with his *De rerum natura*, one can thus read "that other earths exist, in other places, / With varied tribes of men and breeds of beasts" (*On the Nature of the Universe*, trans. Ronald Melville [Oxford: Oxford World Classics, 1999], 66).

Kepler's "Endymionides" get their name from Endymion, who, in Greek mythology, was a young man cherished by Selene (the Moon). In *The Dream, or Lunar Astronomy* (published posthumously in 1634, trans. Edward Rosen [Madison: University of Wisconsin Press, 1967], 151, translation modified) it is effectively a question of "towns on the moon": "Those lunar hollows, first noticed by Galileo, chiefly mark the moonspots, that is, as I show, depressed places in the flat area of the surface, as the seas are among us. But from the shape of the hollows I conclude that those places are, I would say, swampy. And in them the Endymionides usually measure out the areas of their towns."

5. Immanuel Kant, *Universal Natural History and Theory of the Heavens*, trans. Olaf Reinhardt, in *Natural Science*, ed. Eric Watkins (Cambridge: Cambridge University Press, 2012).

6. As Jean Seidengart remarks in a note to the French translation (*Histoire générale de la nature et Théorie du ciel* [Paris: Vrin, 1984], 198), this is indeed a reference to Huygens, even if the passage Kant cites is nowhere to be found in the *Kosmotheoros*.

7. Bernard Le Bovier de Fontenelle, *Conversations on the Plurality of Worlds*, trans. H. A. Hargreaves (Berkeley: University of California Press, 1990), 25.

8. Ibid., 45.

9. Immanuel Kant, *Conflict of the Faculties*, trans. Mary J. Gregor and Robert Anchor, in *Religion and Rational Theology*, ed. Allen W. Wood and George di Giovanni (Cambridge: Cambridge University Press, 2001), 297.

10. In this context, one should remember the history of the word *revolution* itself. Its origin is astronomical (Copernicus's 1543 *De revolutionibus orbium coelestium*), as Hannah Arendt convincingly demonstrated (*On Revolution* [New York: Penguin, 1990]). The Kantian analogies between the cycles of the planets and the course of human affairs that we read particularly in "The Idea for a Universal History from a Cosmopolitan Point of View," participate in this history of the word.

11. Peter Fenves (in *Late Kant: Towards Another Law of the Earth* [London: Routledge, 2003]) has devoted remarkable analyses to the "terrestrial revolutions" envisaged by Kant and to their causes or warning signs (earthquakes, atmospheric electricity, climatic cooling). By starting with Fenves's fine book—which these pages have encountered on many points—one could construct something like a Kantian thinking of ecology *avant la lettre*.

12. Immanuel Kant, "Answer to the Question: What Is Enlightenment," in *Political Writings*, 55. *Aufklarung*, writes Kant in §40 of his Third Critique, is "liberation from superstition," 174.

13. Immanuel Kant, *Toward Perpetual Peace* (1795), trans. H. B. Nisbet, in *Political Writings*, 125.

14. Immanuel Kant, *Anthropology from a Pragmatic Point of View* (Cambridge: Cambridge University Press, 2006), 237.

15. Fontenelle, *Conversations on the Plurality of Worlds,* 57.

16. Immanuel Kant, *Observations on the Feeling of the Beautiful and Sublime and Other Writings*, trans. Paul Guyer in Immanuel Kant, *Anthropology, History, and Education*, ed. Günter Zöller and Robert B. Louden (Cambridge: Cambridge University Press, 2007), 23.

17. See Carl Schmitt, *Land und Meer: Eine weltgeschichtliche Betrachtung* (1942; Stuttgart: Klett-Cotta, 2008), 7: "Man is an earthly being [*Landwesen*]; he walks on land [*Landtreter*]. He stands, walks and moves on firm earth. This is his standpoint and his ground [*sein Standpunkt und sein Boden*]; and this is what gives him his point of view [*Blickpunkt*]; it is what determines his impressions and his way of seeing the world."

18. The beautiful is play between imagination and understanding: "The subjective universal communicability of the kind of representation in a judgment of taste, since it is supposed to occur without presupposing a determinate concept, can be nothing other than the state of mind in the free play of the imagination and the understanding" (§9, 148); "the aesthetic power of judgment in judging the beautiful relates the imagination in its free play to the understanding, in order to agree with its concepts in general (without determination of them)" (§26, 139).

19. "Être-là-bas: Phénoménologie et orientation" (Being-out-there: Phenomenology and orientation) is the title of a fine essay Bernard Stiegler devoted to Husserl's reflections on the Earth, planets, and the cosmos (*Alter*, no. 4 [1996]: 263–77). We will come back to this.

20. The expression is Kant's and comes from the second section of his "philosophical sketch" called *Perpetual Peace* (*Political Writings*, 105): "Third Definitive Article of a Perpetual Peace: Cosmopolitan Right shall be limited to Conditions of Universal Hospitality."

21. In the double sense of the word *cosmos* (guise and world) as of its Latin equivalent *mundus*. See Jaan Puhvel, "The Origins of the Greek Kosmos and Latin Mundus," *American Journal of Philology* 97, no. 2 (1976): 154–67.

22. Jacques Rancière, *The Politics of Aesthetics: The Distribution of the Sensible*, trans. Gabriel Rockhill (New York: Continuum, 2004), 13.

In *Men in Black II*, the sequel directed by Barry Sonnenfeld in 2002, there is a giant neurolyzer on the Statue of Liberty that erases the memories of all New Yorkers.

23. See the distinction Rancière proposes in "Wrong: Politics and Police," a chapter of *Disagreement: Politics and Philosophy*, trans. Julie Rose (Minneapolis: University of Minnesota Press, 1999), 28.

24. Siegfried Kracauer, *Der Detektiv-Roman: Ein philosophischer Traktat,* in *Werke,* vol. 1, ed. Inka Mülder-Bach (Frankfurt am Main: Suhrkamp, 2006).

25. In *Rogues: Two Essays on Reason* (trans. Pascale-Anne Brault and Michael Naas [Stanford: Stanford University Press, 2005]), Jacques Derrida, while wondering about reason yet to come (142), concedes to a kind of Copernican trembling of deconstruction; commenting on Husserl's *Crisis of European Sciences*, he wonders: "Can one really replace the sun? Can one think an original technical prosthesis of the sun?" (140). Right before affirming that deconstruction is "an unconditional rationalism" (142), Derrida will thus—and at a particular, perhaps unique moment of his oeuvre—have opened this cosmotheoretical horizon: changing suns, taking one solar system for another.

4. Weightless: The Archimedean Point of the Sensible

1. *Men in Black,* dir. Barry Sonnenfeld (1997).

2. See Hannah Arendt, *The Human Condition* (Chicago: University of Chicago Press, 1989), 262–68.

3. It must be repeated: It is Jacques Rancière who, starting at least with *Disagreement*, has unfolded a strong political reading of Kantian aesthetics (which owes more than it might want to admit to Hannah Arendt, see above, chapter 1, note 9). With explicit reference to Kant's *Critique of the Power of Judgment* and defining the aesthetic as the "distribution [*partage*] of the sensible," Rancière writes, "That a palace may be the object of an evaluation that has no bearing on the convenience of a residence, the privileges of a role, or the emblems of a majesty, is what, for Kant, particularizes the aesthetic community and the requirement of universality proper to it. So the autonomization of aesthetics means . . . constituting a kind of community of sense experience that works on the assumption of the 'as if' that includes those who are not included by

revealing a mode of existence of sense experience that has eluded the allocation of parties and lots. There never has been any 'aestheticization' of politics in the modern age because politics is aesthetic in principle" (*Disagreement: Politics and Philosophy*, trans. Julie Rose [Minneapolis: University of Minnesota Press, 1999], 57–58). In *The Politics of Aesthetics: The Distribution of the Sensible*, trans. Gabriel Rockhill (New York: Continuum, 2004), Rancière speaks of "politics as a form of experience": "This aesthetics . . . can be understood in a Kantian sense—re-examined perhaps by Foucault—as the system of *a priori* forms determining what presents itself to sense experience. It is a delimitation of spaces and times, of the visible and the invisible, of speech and noise" (13). During a recent interview ("Les territoires de la pensée partagée," 2007, reprinted in *Et tant pis pour les gens fatigués: Entretiens* (Paris: Editions Amsterdam, 2009), 582, 584), Rancière mobilizes the category of "anyone" in a way that immediately recalls the *jedermann* in Kant's Third Critique.

4. Schmitt is perhaps closer to a certain aspect of Kant's posterity than he thinks when, in "Appropriation/ Distribution/Production," he writes that "the meaning of *nomos* . . . is an *Ur-teil* [an original division] and its outcome" (Carl Schmitt, *The Nomos of the Earth*, trans. G. L. Ulmen (1950; New York: Telos, 2003), 326). In German, *Urteil* does in effect mean judgment; and Schmittean discourse on *nomos* could very well imply or initiate a "critique of the power of judgment" (*Kritik der Urteilskraft*) as, quite precisely, a division of the sensible. (On the false etymology—of which Fichte, Hegel, and Hölderlin take advantage—that holds that *Urteil* is a primary division, *ursprünglich teilen*, one can consult Manfred Frank's remarks in *The Philosophical Foundations of Early German Romanticism* (Albany: State University of New York Press, 2004), 85, 103).

5. The second part of the title "Foundational Investigations of the Phenomenological Origin of the Spatiality of Nature: The Originary Ark, the Earth, Does Not Move" (trans. Fred Kersten, rev. Leonard Lawlor in Maurice Merleau-Ponty, *Husserl at the Limits of Phenomenology,* edited by Leonard Lawlor with Bettina Bergo [Chicago: Northwestern University Press, 2001], 117–31) is borrowed from the remarks on the cover of the manuscript: "*Reversal of Copernican Doctrine (Umsturz der kopernikanischen Lehre)* in the interpretation

of the habitual vision of the world. The originary ark, the Earth, does not move. Foundational investigations of the phenomenological origin of corporeity, the spatiality of nature in the primary sense of the natural sciences." This remarkable cosmotheoretical meditation is in effect an exception among the passing mentions of a possible cosmic point of view in the work of other thinkers. I have in mind in particular Hannah Arendt and the "watcher from the universe" who suddenly pops up in the final pages of *The Human Condition*: "It at once becomes manifest that all [the] activities [of man], watched from a sufficiently removed vantage point in the universe, would appear not as activities of any kind but as processes, so that, as a scientist recently put it, modern motorization would appear like a process of biological mutation in which human bodies gradually begin to be covered by shells of steel. For the watcher from the universe, this mutation would be no more or less mysterious than the mutation which now goes on before our eyes in those small living organisms which we fought with antibiotics and which mysteriously have developed new strains to resist us" (322–23). Arendt also considers the hypothesis of "an emigration of men from the earth to some other planet" (10) but, in one incidental remark that seems to recognize the importance of science fiction, she quickly reduces its role to a simple literary expression of earthly desires and affects: "The highly non-respectable literature of science fiction (to which, unfortunately, nobody yet has paid the attention it deserves as a *vehicle of mass sentiments and mass desires*)" (2, emphasis mine). One might also mention the "apologue of the Martian" in book 2 of Lacan's *Seminar* (trans. Sylvana Tomaselli [Cambridge: Cambridge University Press, 1988]), in which Lacan also mentions the *topos* of "the point of view of Sirius" to characterize "the manner in which man comes into [*s'intéresse*] . . . speech" (283).

6. Schmitt, as Günter Maschke indicates in a note in his monumental collection of Schmitt's work in *Frieden oder Pazifismus? Arbeiten zum Völkerrecht und zur internationalen Politik, 1924–1978* (Berlin: Duncker und Humblot, 2005), read science fiction novels "in which inhabitants of faraway stars considered invading the Earth, so much so that the question was posed as to the unification of humanity faced with this kind of extrapolitical enemy [*gegen einen solchen aussenpolitischen Feind*]" (232). Among others, Schmitt had

read John Wyndham's *The Chrysalids* (1955), and one understands why since in its German translation, the novel had the inviting title of *Wem gehört die Erde?* "To whom does the Earth belong?"

7. "There was once," writes Nietzsche in "On the Pathos of Truth" (trans. Taylor Carman, in *On Truth and Untruth* [New York: Harper Collins, 2010], 13), "there was once a star on which some clever animals invented *knowledge*. It was the most arrogant, most mendacious minute in world history, but it was only a minute. After nature caught its breath a little, the star froze, and the clever animals had to die." Husserl ups the stakes, as we just read, with the "entropy" of earth. This "fiction of the total annihilation of the world" may well be, as Derrida suggested in a previously cited interview ("Scènes des differences," in *Littérature*, no. 142 [June 2006]) "the very element of philosophical discourse."

8. See Jean-Luc Nancy, *Le poids d'une pensée* (Grenoble: Griffon d'Argile and Presses Universitaires de Grenoble, 1991).

9. Italo Calvino, "The Distance of the Moon," in *Cosmicomics*, trans. William Weaver (New York: Harcourt Brace Jovanovich, 1976), 3–18.

10. I am of course alluding to the (overly) famous characterization of the aura given by Walter Benjamin in "The Work of Art in the Age of Its Technical Reproducibility": "the unique apparition of a distance, however near it may be" (third version, 1939, trans. Harry Zohn and Edmund Jephcott, in *Selected Writings*, vol. 4, ed. Howard Eiland and Michael W. Jennings [Cambridge: Harvard University Press, 2003], 255). In the first published version of the same text (1935), Benjamin spoke of "a strange tissue of time and space" (*Selected Writings*, 3:104). Rather than interpreting the aura, as it has been too often, on the horizon of its loss (the claimed loss of uniqueness, attributable to mechanical, photographic, or filmic reproduction), it will be necessary to show just how much film, for Benjamin, *opens* the possibility of an auratic experience that he is not far from describing in cosmotheoretical, even cosmopolitical terms: "Our bars and city streets, our offices and furnished rooms, our railroad stations and our factories seemed to close relentlessly around us. Then came film and exploded this prison-world with the dynamite of the split second, so that now we can set off calmly on journeys of adventure among its far-flung debris. With the close-up,

space expands, with slow motion, movement is extended. And just as enlargement not merely clarifies what we see indistinctly 'in any case,' but brings to light entirely new structures of matter, slow motion not only reveals familiar aspects of movements, but discloses quite unknown aspects within them—aspects 'which do not appear as the retarding of natural movements but have curious gliding, floating character of their own'" (*Selected Writings*, 4:265–66; Benjamin is citing Rudolf Arnheim, *Film as Art* [Berkeley: University of California Press, 1957]). Rather than concluding, with Benjamin himself, that "it is another nature which speaks to the camera as compared to the eye" (Benjamin, *Selected Writings*, 4:266), here I have wanted to suggest, with Kant or beyond Kant, that the radical alterity that surfaces in the cinematographic gaze is at bottom the same one that already inhabits any point of view as such. But inscribing within this *as such* a philosofictive *as if*.

11. See Sergei Eisenstein, *Le Mouvement de l'art*, ed. François Albéra and Naoum Kleiman (Paris: Editions du Cerf, 1986), 77.

12. As if here, in this clownish register of farce, there were a memory of the affinity between cosmologics and cosmetics.

13. H. G. Wells, *The War of the Worlds* (1898; Rockville, Md.: Arc Manor, 2008), 124.

14. Benjamin, *Selected Writings*, 4:262 (TN: translation modified).

Postface: What's Left of Cosmopolitanism?

1. The epigraph is from Jacques Derrida, *On Cosmopolitanism and Forgiveness*, trans. Mark Dooley and Michael Hughes (New York: Routledge, 2001), 3. [TN: translation modified for accuracy. Szendy also gives a reading of the original French title of Derrida's essay ("Cosmopolites de tous les pays, encore un effort!"), which is translated by Dooley simply as "On Cosmopolitanism."]

2. See http://www.mlwerke.de/me. If there are ultimately few occurrences of the signifier *cosmopolitan* under Marx's plume, the ones there are speak for themselves. One could also cite *The German Ideology*: "Free competition and world trade gave birth to hypocritical, bourgeois cosmopolitanism and the notion of man" (*den heuchlerischen, bürgerlichen Kosmopolitismus und den Begriff des Menschen*).

3. Jacques Derrida, *Adieu to Emmanuel Levinas*, trans. Pascale-Anne Brault and Michael Naas (Stanford: Stanford University Press, 1999), 88.

4. Giuseppe Mazzini, "Nationality and Cosmopolitanism" (first published in English in 1847 in the *People's Journal* in London), in *A Cosmopolitanism of Nations: Giuseppe Mazzini's Writings on Democracy, National Building, and International Relations*, ed. Stefano Recchia and Nadia Urbinati (Princeton: Princeton University Press, 2009), 57.

5. See Marcel Mauss, "La nation et l'internationalisme" (1920), in *Oeuvres* (Paris: Minuit, 1969), 3:626–34. Mauss's discourse is close to Mazzini's: "Internationalism worthy of the name is the opposite of cosmopolitanism. It does not deny the nation. It situates it. Internation is the opposite of a-nation. It is also consequently the opposite of nationalism, which isolates the nation" (TN: translation mine).

6. G. W. F. Hegel, *Elements of the Philosophy of Right*, trans. H. B. Nisbet (Cambridge: Cambridge University Press, 1991), 240. In 1802–3, in *Natural Law*, trans. T. M. Knox (Philadelphia: University of Pennsylvania Press, 1975, 132), Hegel noted that philosophy "cannot . . . escape into the shapelessness of cosmopolitanism, still less into the void of the Rights of Man, or the like void of a league of nations or a world republic. These are abstractions and formalisms filled with exactly the opposite of ethical vitality."

7. Marcel Mauss, *La nation* (1920), in *Oeuvres*, 3:573–625 (TN: translation mine).

8. Derrida, *On Cosmopolitanism and Forgiveness*, 22.

9. In *Un monde commun: Pour une cosmo-politique des conflits* (Paris: Seuil, 2003), Etienne Tassin retains from Derrida only his reading of the "paradox" at work in the Kantian notion of universal hospitality (174–75).

10. Immanuel Kant, *Anthropology from a Pragmatic Point of View* (Cambridge: Cambridge University Press, 2006), 236.

11. In particular in Jacques Derrida, *The Animal That Therefore I Am*, trans. David Wills (New York: Fordham University Press, 2008).

12. On Diogenes of Sinope, see Diogenes Laertius, *Lives of Eminent Philosophers*, trans. R. D. Hicks (Cambridge: Harvard University Press,

1979), 6.63. This tradition will continue through Seneca and Marcus Aurelius.

13. Cicero, *On Moral Ends*, ed. Julia Annas, trans. Raphael Woolf (Cambridge: Cambridge University Press, 2001), 85–86.

14. Augustine, *The City of God Against the Pagans*, trans. R. W. Dyson (Cambridge: Cambridge University Press, 1998), 940.

15. Ibid., 945.

16. Jacques Derrida, *The Beast and the Sovereign*, trans. Geoffrey Bennington (Chicago: University of Chicago Press, 2011), 2:8–9.

17. Jacques Derrida, "Rams: Uninterrupted Dialogue—Between Two Infinities, the Poem," in *Sovereignties in Question: The Poetics of Paul Celan*, trans. Thomas Dutoit (New York: Fordham University Press, 2005), 158.

18. The cosmopolitanism to come can therefore not be described in Etienne Tassin's terms when he translates the notion of "worldlessness" in Hannah Arendt as "acosmisme" (Tassin, *Un monde commun*, 17 and passim): "Cosmopolitics," he writes, "is first of all resistance to acosmism" (translation mine). Hegel, particularly in the *Science of Logic* that composes the first part of his *Encyclopaedia of the Philosophical Sciences* (§50 in the 1830 edition), speaks of Spinoza's "acosmism" according to which "the world is determined . . . as a mere phenomenon without genuine reality. See G. W. F. Hegel, *The Encylopaedia Logic*, trans. Theodore F. Geraets, W. A. Suchting, and H. S. Harris (Indianapolis: Hackett, 1991), 97.

19. *Die Erde ercheint als die Unwelt der Irrnis. Sie ist seyngeschichtlich der Irrstern.* See Martin Heidegger, "Overcoming Metaphysics," in *The End of Philosophy*, trans. Joan Stambaugh (New York: Harper and Row, 1973), 109. The German verb *irren* is related to the latin *errare.*

20. Heidegger, *End of Philosophy*, 107–8.

21. Martin Heidegger, "The Way to Language," in *On the Way to Language*, trans. Peter D. Hertz (New York: Harper, 1971). The first of the three conferences was held in Fribourg on December 4, 1957, two months to the day after the launch of the first *Sputnik* on October 4.

22. Emmanuel Levinas, "Heidegger, Gagarin, and Us," first published in *Information juive*, no. 131 (1961), trans. Seàn Hand in *Difficult Freedom: Essays on Judaism* (Baltimore: Johns Hopkins University, 1997), 231–34.

23. Ibid., 232–33.

24. Geoffrey Bennington and Jacques Derrida, *Jacques Derrida* (Chicago: University of Chicago Press, 1999), 134–35.
25. The you to whom the planetizing address is sent, we read in "Rams," "can designate a living being, a human or non-human animal" and "can also be addressed to the dead, to the survivor or to the specter" (Derrida, "Rams," 159).